P9-CEG-673

Hats
&
Eyeglasses

Hats
&
Eyeglasses

◆ A FAMILY LOVE AFFAIR WITH GAMBLING ◆

Martha Frankel

JEREMY P. TARCHER/PENGUIN

a member of Penguin Group (USA) Inc.

New York

JEREMY P. TARCHER/PENGUIN
Published by the Penguin Group
Penguin Group (USA) Inc., 375 Hudson Street, New York, New York 10014,
USA • Penguin Group (Canada), 90 Eglinton Avenue East, Suite 700, Toronto,
Ontario M4P 2Y3, Canada (a division of Pearson Penguin Canada Inc.) •
Penguin Books Ltd, 80 Strand, London WC2R 0RL, England • Penguin Ireland,
25 St Stephen's Green, Dublin 2, Ireland (a division of Penguin Books Ltd) •
Penguin Group (Australia), 250 Camberwell Road, Camberwell, Victoria 3124, Australia
(a division of Pearson Australia Group Pty Ltd) • Penguin Books India Pvt Ltd,
11 Community Centre, Panchsheel Park, New Delhi–110 017, India • Penguin Group (NZ),
67 Apollo Drive, Rosedale, North Shore 0632, New Zealand (a division of Pearson
New Zealand Ltd) • Penguin Books (South Africa) (Pty) Ltd, 24 Sturdee Avenue,
Rosebank, Johannesburg 2196, South Africa

Penguin Books Ltd, Registered Offices:
80 Strand, London WC2R 0RL, England

Most Tarcher/Penguin books are available at special quantity discounts for
bulk purchase for sales promotions, premiums, fund-raising, and educational needs.
Special books or book excerpts also can be created to fit specific needs.
For details, write Penguin Group (USA) Inc. Special Markets,
375 Hudson Street, New York, NY 10014.

Library of Congress Cataloging-in-Publication Data

Frankel, Martha.
Hats & eyeglasses : a family love affair with gambling / Martha Frankel.
p.   cm.
ISBN 978-1-58542-558-7
1. Frankel, Martha.   2. Gamblers—United States—Biography.
3. Gambling—United States.   I. Title.   II. Title: Hats and eyeglasses.
HV6710.3.F73   2008   2007044949
363.4'2092—dc22
[B]

Printed in the United States of America
1   3   5   7   9   10   8   6   4   2

BOOK DESIGN BY AMANDA DEWEY

Some of the names and identifying characteristics have been changed to protect the privacy of the
individuals involved.

For my father, Marty Frankel, who taught me that numbers are the one constant in this world, explained the difference between a passed ball and a wild pitch, and believed I was his lucky charm.

For Uncle Benny, who showed me how to thread a worm on a hook, pour a really stiff drink, and sear a pork chop to perfection, all while wearing lime-green leisure pants.

For Aunt Tillie, the greatest cook and role model. You always said you were more interesting than the people I was interviewing—so no rolling over in your grave.

And for my mother, Sylvia Frankel, who said that every story has a thousand angles, and that it's all in the telling. And who gave me the best poker advice—*It's not the seat, it's the ass in it.*

♦ CONTENTS ♦

Hats
&
Eyeglasses

ONE

Hats & Eyeglasses

This is how I remember things: my mother was in the kitchen with her girlfriends. I had just turned four. I know this because my Aunt Tillie kept kissing my face and shrieking, "Four years old—what a big girl!"

The women were passing around photos, pictures of themselves taken on a trip a few months earlier. "Why didn't you tell me I was so fat?" they asked each other with genuine surprise. They ran to the mirror, craning to see if the pictures were lying. They started hooting with laughter. My mother said, "Stop, or I'll pee in my pants," but that only made them laugh harder. She did, too, and had to change her clothes. Nobody was embarrassed.

The kitchen was ablaze with light. They went in and

sat down to play mah-jongg. They said, "One crack," "Two bam," "Did you hear that Jack left Bess?" And then there was silence while everyone regrouped. They made plans to bring Bess some food, to take her out shopping, to "throw that bum's clothes out on the street." These women would fill her life with so much love that it would numb her to the loss of this no-good-nik.

The women came dressed up for these Friday-night games, but by the time they sat down to play they had changed into their uniforms: housecoats that snapped down the front. During the course of the evening, at least one of them would rip open her housecoat and cry, "Is it hot in here or is it me?"

My mother had food on the counter—bagels and cream cheese, egg salad with bits of bacon, tuna salad thick with mayonnaise. There were pineapples that had been cut into quarters, little Chinese umbrellas stuck in them so they looked like riverboats. The women called me *Cookie*, and tried to entice me with treats. They put food on the end of their fingers and held them out to me, human lollipops, all for my pleasure. They lifted my shirt and kissed my belly, their love for me total and unconditional.

I call all these women *Aunts* and their husbands *Uncles*, even though they aren't, because this is who I think of as family. My mother and Aunt Tillie were like two sides of the same coin. They weren't sisters but friends since they were five, when their mothers met on the bench at Poe Park on the Grand Concourse. As their mothers fed the pigeons and read *The Forvitz*, the Yiddish newspaper, the girls played in the bandshell. My mother was soft-spoken and gracious; Tillie had a voice like a trucker, with a vocabulary to match. When I got older and liked a boy who was going away for the summer, my mother said, gently, "Absence makes the heart grow fonder." Without missing a beat, Tillie growled, "Out of sight, out of mind." They bickered and argued, but watch out if you got between them: they would both go for your throat. The mah-jongg women knew this—they were girls back there on the Grand Concourse, too—and watched their step around the two of them.

My father was playing poker with the husbands in the living room. There was a standing lamp in the corner and a bottle of Crown Royal and some shot glasses on a snack table. The men smoked cigars and said things like, "You're killing me," or, "You sure stepped in shit tonight." It was friendly, but with a little something added that I didn't recognize.

The men called each other by their nicknames—the Major, who was in the army reserve; Cha Cha, who was a world-class dancer; Broadway, who worked in the garment district and was grossly overweight but had the most delicate hands; Sammy B, a bachelor friend from the old days, always in a good mood, always bringing packages to my mother because they fell off the truck; and Unc, Tillie's husband Ben, who acted like he was everyone's long-lost relative. They called my father The Pencil, because he was a CPA and had a head for numbers.

Sometimes, when I skipped around the poker table, the men would ask me to get them a bite to eat. I prided myself on the beautiful plates I'd make for them. *The usual* from Broadway meant a bagel with a *schmear.* They'd also ask me to change the channel on the television that droned in the corner. And every once in a while one of them would bend down to show me their cards. They'd shake their heads in disgust, and I knew to sigh back at them. My father would lift me in the air and say, "Sit here with me, sweetie, I could use some luck." When he won, he nuzzled me with his stubbly face.

One night Broadway moaned, "I've got hats and eyeglasses." The other men murmured in empathy. I scrambled over to see what that meant. I looked at his cards, but I didn't see any hats, or any eyeglasses.

"It's what happens when a ship goes down, and everything sinks," Broadway told me, lifting me onto his immense lap. "What floats to the surface is hats and eyeglasses. It means I have crapola, that I don't have a prayer."

I looked at his cards and saw that Broadway had missed

something. "But you have three A's," I said, so proud of myself.

The men all threw their cards down on the table and laughed. "Whew, that could have cost me," my father said with a big grin. Unc handed me a quarter, and all the men followed his lead. I was thrilled by the coins, and held my hand out to Broadway. But he was furious and set me down so roughly I fell.

"Give the kid a quarter," my father said as I straightened up. "Like hell," Broadway mumbled. I thought I'd done the wrong thing, but my father looked at me so lovingly that I did a somersault and almost choked on the sourball in my mouth. I stood there, sputtering and trying to catch my breath.

"Don't scare the baby," my mother said, coming in to see what the fuss was about. She picked me up and started back to the kitchen. But I wasn't scared. I liked it out there with the men. I liked the feel of the cards, the sound of the money hitting the table, the look they got when they won. I wriggled out of her arms and climbed back on my father's lap. "Three things you should always remember," he whispered in my ear. "*If you don't have anything, get out. If you're second best, get out. But if you've got the goods, make them pay.*" I didn't have a clue what this meant, but I nodded my head as he kissed my ear.

◆ ◆ ◆

We were living in the Bronx then, in what was called *the Projects*, the low-income city housing. I loved it there. All the mothers, like mine, stayed home, the fathers went off to their offices, and we had hundreds of friends within half a block. My sister, Helene, and I shared an enormous room. We were shocked when my parents came and told us we were moving. I was eight, Helene fourteen. Helene started flinging herself around our room, crying and shrieking that she couldn't leave, *wouldn't* leave. I did the same, not because I was upset about the move, but because the flinging and crying seemed so grown-up. My parents kept insisting that this was a good thing, that this is what people did—move to a place with more opportunity.

They offered us two choices: we could move to Yonkers, buy a house where we would have our own bedrooms and we would be close to my father's pinochle group and their families. Or we could get a condo in Queens, share a bedroom, and we'd be near Aunt Tillie and the mah-jongg women and poker men.

Helene and I secretly chose Queens, but for months we let my parents schlep us all around Yonkers, where we looked at big houses and told them we would make up our minds *soon*. Helene was hoping they would forget about the move, but my parents kept talking about more and more opportunities.

Queens turned out to be wonderful. Our new room was smaller, but it had a great big window that looked out toward where the 1963 World's Fair and that enormous Unisphere were being built. The neighborhood also had hundreds of kids my age, and this apartment seemed to make my parents so proud. They hired a decorator, who was really my mother's new beautician, and filled the apartment with salmon-colored couches and chairs and gold-leaf mirrors. The furniture had thick plastic covers that never came off and were especially sticky and hot in the summer. We understood that what was under that plastic was to be preserved—not ruined by our scabby legs or Oreo crumbs.

My father went into business for himself, and set up his office in the house. He was always home, and had lots of time for me whenever I came in from school or the playground. My mother took a job as a bookkeeper at the local temple, and even though our family wasn't religious, we became good friends with the rabbi and his wife, and had them over for dinner all the time. "Hide the bacon," my mother would joke when they knocked on the door. And although Helene sulked for the first year, she made friends and seemed to settle into this land of more opportunities.

On Sundays the whole gang met at Tillie and Unc's. Tillie cooked huge meals—pea soup with flanken, fried veal cutlets, lasagna with giant pieces of sausage. All the aunts and uncles had children who were near my age. We referred to each other as cousins and became best friends. We kids crowded around Tillie, waiting for a taste, wanting just to be near her. She made blenders full of daiquiris, and let us slurp some before we brought the glasses out to our fathers. She taught us to say *shit*, and never tired of hearing us try to use it in a sentence. She let us do all the things our mothers said not to, and made us feel safe while we did them.

Our mothers whispered to each other about how Tillie and Unc couldn't have children. Couldn't? Why would they want to? They were so much more glamorous than our parents. Unc worked at Idlewild Airport, in a job he described as top secret. When we were flying somewhere, he would meet us and whisk us to the front of the line. Tillie was one of the top salespeople at R&K Dresses. She was adored at work, surrounded by homosexuals and Christian Scientists, people who sought her opinion on everything. I never saw her wear the same thing twice. She made more money than anyone else in my parents' group and, because she didn't have children of her own, she spoiled us all with extravagant gifts.

The uncles would be in the living room, watching

sports, yelling at the screen and at each other. There were three televisions lined up next to each other on Tillie's buffet: it wasn't unusual for them to be watching three baseball, basketball, or football games at the same time. When I wandered by, Unc would offer me a dime to turn the sound up on TV 1, down on TV 2, and adjust the color on TV 3. When remote controls first came out, the uncles bought all new televisions, but they were infuriated when they realized that almost anything, from the jingling of change in their pockets to a ray of sunlight, could set off the remotes and get the channels rolling. They badgered Zenith until the company eventually replaced dozens of clickers.

After dinner, the men would go into the extra bedroom to play poker. They still called it Sammy B's room, although he hadn't lived with Tillie and Unc for over a decade. They lit their cigars and counted out their money. The boys tried to push past me to get closer to the poker table. They were never invited to sit on a lap, and they resented me for that, knowing I didn't really care about the game. I was too busy entertaining, trying to make the men laugh, telling jokes and singing songs. I walked around with plates of cookies, and the men gave me tips, which I handed over to my father, the CPA, who put them in the bank and told me that not only was I smart and beautiful, I was rich, too. I didn't really care when Unc or the Major explained how you should stay in with two high pair, or why you should bet slowly when you had the winning hand. But the boys were listening. They didn't miss a word.

While I was in Sammy B's room, the girls were standing at Tillie's side, trying to master the right amount of oil to put in kasha varnishkas. "A lot," Helene told me on the way home. The girls learned to play canasta, knit scarves, sew a running stitch.

I learned to read the *Daily Racing Form*. Not for nothing was I The Pencil's little girl. For years we had played number games when I couldn't fall asleep. My father would climb into my bed, and I would lie with my back to him, eyes wide open, almost daring him to get me to relax. "Count forwards from 1 by threes," he'd say, pushing the length of his leg into my back and rubbing my neck, "and backwards from 99 by sevens." An orphan, my father loved Helene and me with complete devotion, saying every day how he would "swim the English Channel" for us.

"Okay," I'd say, annoyed that he thought he could trick me so easily. "One, 99, 4, 92 . . . 7, 85, 10 . . . 78?" And then my feet would seem to rise above my head and I'd drift off into an exhausted sleep.

When I was about eight, and I could do the numbers game without falling asleep, he taught me about prime numbers. We'd start with the easy ones—1, 2, 3, 5, 7, 11, 13. On and on, until we were into triple digits. We'd get so excited when we found a new one. "How about 479?" I shrieked one night after we had been stuck on 417 for weeks. My mother came in to make sure everything was okay. He left me there, numbers jumping through my head like lions through a hoop, and I felt a mixture of excitement and resentment: What could they possibly have to talk about that was more interesting than this?

So, when I was ten and my mother needed to run out and do a little shopping at Loehmann's, it seemed completely natural that I would go to the track with my father. While Unc maneuvered his huge Cadillac convertible through traffic, I sat on my father's lap as he held up the *Racing Form* and explained what all those little numbers meant: dates the horses had run before, how they finished, the time the winner had run, the type of race, how the horse seemed in his last outing (tired, lagging), the odds, the jockeys. He explained the difference between *trotters,* where the jockey sits behind the horse in a little buggy called a sulky, and *flats,* where the jockey rides on the horse.

That first night at Yonkers Raceway I was fascinated: outside, bums begged for spare change while women in short skirts said "Hiya, honey" to men they didn't even know. "Don't stare," my father warned, but I couldn't help it. Inside, it was all cigar smoke and harsh talk. My father and Unc had friends here, men I'd never heard about:

Skelly, the unluckiest bookie in the world; the Fat Man, who couldn't have weighed more than a hundred pounds soaking wet; Pumpkin, who had a big head and a change dispenser on his belt like an ice-cream man, handing out quarters to anyone who did his bidding.

I loved the way the men ripped their losing tickets and tossed them on the floor in distaste: when I reached down to pick one up, Unc grabbed my hand and said, "Don't touch!" as if I were playing with matches. I realized that those discarded tickets were worse than dirt, failed dreams not to be dredged up again.

I started carrying the *Racing Form* in my book bag. I learned about daily doubles and exactas, started to recognize the jockeys from one week to the next, learned the name of the man who sold the tickets, the one who smiled at me and said, "Hope this one's a *big* winner, honey," as he handed the tickets to my father.

My father and my uncles and I went to the Belmont Stakes for the first time on a warm, drizzly, late-spring day. My hair was pulled back in a ponytail, and I had on pink lipstick, the first I ever wore. Most of the crowd was straining to catch a glimpse of former president Dwight Eisenhower and his wife, Mamie, who would be placing the blanket of carnations on the winning horse. But we were Kennedy people, so we stood around with the rest of the railbirds, reading the *Racing Form* under our umbrellas.

As my father was about to bet forty dollars on the favorite, Carry Back, the little colt who had won the Kentucky Derby and the Preakness, I grabbed his arm and said that maybe he should put some money on Sherluck, a 65–1 underdog who had finished fifth in both the Derby and the Preakness.

"Just a little bit faster and he would have been in the money both times," I pointed out. My father looked at me for a long while without saying a word. Finally he nodded and said, "Okay, we'll split the bet, twenty on each." He let me buy the tickets myself, and I bet Sherluck across the board—win, place, and show. I clutched those tickets so tightly that my sweat smudged the numbers that ran across the paper. Sherluck was in second place for most of the race, but didn't disappoint: at the stretch he seemed to find his footing and won by over two lengths. My father and Unc went wild, twirling me and kissing me and telling anyone within earshot what a smart, smart girl I was. Oh, and Carry Back? He came in seventh.

I went with them to the track for years—to Yonkers, Belmont, Roosevelt, wherever the action was. I did my homework while perusing the *Racing Form*. Maybe once or twice a night I'd spot a horse that I thought might be worth a bet; to their constant sorrow, I was not inclined to bet every race. I went through puberty with the sound of men yelling and cursing all around me; had my first kiss in the clubhouse at Belmont, an older boy who pushed me up against the bathroom door, forced his knee between my legs, and panted, "Don't you want to have an orgasm?" I went home and looked it up in the dictionary. It said: *The climax of sexual excitement, marked by the release of tumescence in the erectile organs of both sexes.*

No, thank you.

I got pretty good at picking long shots, and my father let me make my own bets, handing me a twenty-dollar bill as we walked through the gates each week. "Knock 'em dead," he'd say. The men took to calling me the Grecian, in honor of oddsmaker Jimmy the Greek. When one of them was having a bad streak, they'd often come to sit next to me, hoping my picks would help recoup part of the fortune they'd had been losing. They'd tell me their sob stories, and I'd give them my choices grudgingly, making it clear that I expected to be paid handsomely for my information. I made hundreds of dollars at the track—thousands—which my father put into a special bank account. "For college," he'd say proudly when the men handed me a ten or a twenty.

"It's okay," Tillie told my mother when she worried that I was interested in all the wrong things. "She's smart, she's adventurous, she'll do just fine."

The night I got my notice of acceptance from the Bronx High School of Science, my father sat at the table and wept. "Anything you want is going to be possible," he said over and over, holding the letter up in the air as if it were the original Ten Commandments. "You could become *an astronaut* . . ."

I wanted to point out to him that I would have to take the bus for over an hour, go back to the Bronx, that place where opportunities weren't as easy to spot. But I was excited, too, and kept my mouth shut. The next day I cut school for the first time. My friends did it all the time, but I never felt the need, because if once a month or so I told my mother that I didn't want to go to school, she'd pack a lunch and we'd drive two hours north to the Catskills so we could get a massage at her favorite hotel, or we'd pick up Tillie at her office in the city and go to a Broadway show. A musical, if we got really lucky. After, my mother would stop and buy the soundtrack, and we would memorize every word and sing it for weeks. But I was about to become an astronaut, for God's sake, so I cut school and smoked cigarettes and felt completely cool.

When I came home that afternoon, Helene was sitting in the kitchen with a look on her face that I had never seen. I started crying before she even said a word; I couldn't believe I had gotten caught. My first time! Helene started crying, too, and that confused me. It was only one day of school, after all. "Grandma was hit by a truck and killed," she said. I screamed.

My mother was completely unhinged by her mother's death—she couldn't stop crying, and telling stories, and then she would take a sleeping pill and fall asleep for a few hours. When she got up, the cycle would start again. I was both sympathetic and scared witless—I had never seen my mother take more than an aspirin, and had never seen her even remotely out of control. But more was to come: six weeks later, her beloved brother, Milton, had a heart attack and died the same night. A few days later my father passed blood in his urine; eight months later my mother and I stared at each other from opposite ends of his coffin, our world gone blank with grief. He had just turned fifty. Three days later, my mother's father, our sweet Grandpa, died in his sleep at the nursing home where he had gone after my grandmother was hit by the truck. My mother's tears had already dried—she said that if she started weeping again, she would never stop.

I began to worry: maybe no one would take care of me. My uncles tried to reassure me. For my sixteenth birthday they brought me an enormous box, which contained the sailor pants I had been coveting for months. They were thick wool, with buttons that made a U-shape around the stomach. But there were four dozen pairs of the pants—they had apparently fallen off a truck. Broadway urged me to sell the other forty-seven—"That'll be a good birthday present," he said—but the gift sent me into a crying jag that lasted for days. My father would have understood, I thought, that all I wanted was one pair. The uncles never brought me another present, and except for the few times when Unc tried to broach the subject but got too awkward, they never, ever talked to me about my father again.

On Sundays I found myself lying in front of the televisions, not wanting to go near the poker game, not knowing how to be with the women. When we graduated from high school, all my boy cousins became gamblers and bookmakers, always hoping to get me interested in one of their scams. "You'd be such a natural," they'd say. I didn't answer.

My cousins became uncomfortable with me. A few of their fathers had had heart attacks, and when mine died they breathed a collective sigh of relief, as if their fathers were safe, now that the boogeyman had taken mine. They didn't know what to say to me, so they kept silent. Which suited my mood just fine.

I wrote to the Bronx High School of Science to say I wouldn't be coming after all; I couldn't imagine a life of numbers without my father. At Martin Van Buren High, I started cutting school with regularity, and when I did show up I was surly and disruptive. In math class I sat woodenly, pretending not to know what was going on, even though I'd secretly write the right answer on a piece of paper that

I burnt with the tip of my cigarette the minute school was out. The words "not living up to her potential" began to roll off everyone's tongue. My mother and I circled each other like weary boxers—it was like we were on a sinking ship and all we could see was hats and eyeglasses.

TWO

Leaving Home

When my father was two, the local butcher found him wandering around his Lower East Side neighborhood. He was sucking his thumb, his diaper was dirty, he was barefoot. The butcher, who knew my grandmother, picked him up and carried him home. There he found chaos—my grandmother curled in a fetal position on her bed, and my father's brother and five sisters trying to take care of her and each other. Somehow no one had noticed when my father walked out the door, and they were panicked that their secret was out: apparently my grandfather had gone for a pack of cigarettes a few months before and had never come back. My grandmother, who had recently given birth to her seventh child, cracked. The children had been trying to make things seem as normal as possible so they could stay together. But the butcher called the authorities, and they placed all of those Frankel kids in the Hebrew Orphan Asylum in Chelsea. My grandmother was put into a mental institution, where she lived for another sixty years, not knowing where she was nor recognizing her children. My grandfather was never heard from again.

The first time my father told me about the orphanage, I burst into tears. I pictured a dark, horrible place, where children were beaten, or worse. My father used to read aloud to us, from Dickens, and from Elizabeth Barrett Browning's "The Cry of the Children," and those two words, *orphanage* and *asylum*, held terrible secrets. But my father dried my eyes and told me not to be scared, that his orphanage wasn't dark and scary at all. Far from that, he felt at home there and had all of his sisters and his brother around. The staff nurtured and supported him. He stayed at the orphanage till he was eighteen, and left there with a great sense of self.

My father enrolled at City College, and was at the local pool hall one night when his friend Red asked him to go tell Red's girlfriend, Sylvia, that he couldn't see her that night. No one had phones, so my father went to Sylvia's house, and when she opened the door, my father fell in love on the spot.

My mother told us that my father just stood at the door, and didn't say anything for a long time. Her sisters and brother and parents were in the living room, playing cards. "Who's there?" they yelled.

My mother invited him in, and their courtship began the next morning, when she told Red that she couldn't go out with him anymore.

My father, who had craved a solid family his whole life, melded perfectly with my mother's warm, loud, happy one. He always included my grandparents in everything we did, and every summer he rented a bungalow in the Catskills for all of us.

Because my mother had dropped out of high school to get a job during the Depression, she and my father always felt strongly that Helene and I had to go to college and do great things. But after my father died, I could barely imagine where I would go to school, or what I would study once I got there.

I took the easy path and went to the University of Miami, a school where almost everyone but me drove a Corvette, had a trust fund, and went out to dinner every night. I was living on the fifteen dollars a week that my mother sent me. I was a virgin when I arrived, but after a few weeks met the head of the local chapter of SDS (Students for a Democratic Society), a charismatic Jewish guy with an Afro—or an "Isro," as we called it—who could incite and inflame the masses of long-haired kids who looked up to him and wanted to join him in changing the world.

After a few nights of weird fumbling we wound up back at his apartment. We barely had our clothes off before he forced himself between my legs, not caring that I was as dry as a cactus. He came within seconds, and then asked me to type a speech he was giving the next day. He rolled over and started to snore. I sat at the typewriter, blood dripping down my legs, until a rage I had suppressed exploded. I left his notes smeared with blood and walked out.

Since my father's death I had been so worried that my mother would fall apart, that she wouldn't have room in her life for anything but her grief, that I hadn't given in to mine. That rage, the "Why me?" of losing my father, the feeling that I had been cheated of something so precious, bubbled up and spilled out of me like red-hot lava.

At the rally the next day, Isro pointed at me from the podium and said I was not a team player. After my mortification passed, I mentioned to a few key people in the movement that he was a premature ejaculator. He left Miami soon after.

Within a month, I had slept with three other boys. I was no closer to having an orgasm, and had just about given up, when I met a good-looking, smooth-talking guy from Chicago, who told me he was studying to be a dentist, that he had a massive trust fund that he would come into when he was twenty-five, and that his family was just going to love me.

He could make me come with his fingers, his tongue, his penis, his voice. We moved into a funky Coconut Grove bungalow with a beagle puppy that neither of us had the knowledge or the inclination to train.

On Sundays he would wake up at seven and begin chopping garlic, dicing peppers, grating onions. He'd add canned tomatoes, fresh basil that he grew in a big pot on the terrace, and cook a sauce that would rival Mama Leone's. He'd make garlic bread and prepare antipasto. We'd sit in front of the television all day long and watch football, baseball, whatever was in season. The phone would ring all the time, guys calling to lay bets or just chat about the games. It felt as if I'd never left home.

With sauce still dripping down his fingers, he'd lay me across the dining table and caress and rub me until I would scream and quiver. Of course I married him.

His parents refused to come to the wedding—they said I wasn't good enough for their golden boy. The irony was not lost on me; the father was a vicious, uneducated bookie, a bully who scared everyone around him. Not long after we married, I found out that my husband wasn't studying to be a dentist—he was on the verge of failing most of his classes. Oh, that trust fund? These were people who kept all their cash in a safe under the bathroom vanity.

Besides the food, sex, and sports, we had nothing in common. When I mentioned that I'd love to live in the country, he laughed and talked about an imaginary apartment in New York City. When he told me he wanted at least three children, I started to panic. And when he got busted for selling cocaine to an undercover agent—fifteen pounds of it—I knew it was time to run away from this mess.

But how do you leave your husband right before he goes to jail?

In my family, it works this way: a "cousin" moved to Miami with her husband, and on a drunken, moonlit night, we slept with each other's husbands. In a stroke of sheer luck, she fell in love with mine.

I left Miami after he had been sentenced to two to four years, but before he started serving his time. I moved to the country, to Woodstock, New York. I got a job as the cashier at the Joyous Lake, the hottest club in town, where musicians like Taj Mahal and Bonnie Raitt were considered house bands. I slept around, drank too much, took drugs with names I couldn't even pronounce, and felt my life slipping away.

After a year or so, during the baseball play-offs, I met Steve. It turned out that we had grown up just miles apart in Queens, went to the same high school, and both came from strong, devoted families, although his didn't think of Las Vegas as the Holy Land.

We had been flirting at the Joyous Lake, and when he called to ask me to have dinner one night, I asked him the question I had been asking men my entire life: "Aren't you going to watch the game?" This was crunch time; game four between the L.A. Dodgers and the Oakland A's. I had a hundred dollars on the outcome myself.

"Nah," Steve answered. "I don't like football."

I fell in love with him in that instant. That he was hardworking, honest, and sidesplittingly funny was just a bonus; that he didn't care about baseball or football was the deal closer. A man who wouldn't be looking over my ass when we had sex so he could see the box scores was more foreign to me than if he spoke in tongues with snakes slithering around his feet. Everything about him seemed so exotic.

With Steve I started to make the world around me as comfortable, as familiar, as safe as I could. When any of my cousins came by with their crazy schemes, I would take Steve into the bedroom and lay him down on the bed. I'd lick his penis until he was breathless. "If you get involved with them," I'd warn him, right before he came in my mouth, "you'll lose me."

I wasn't like them anymore. They liked to take the easy

way out; I often took the hard road in. They were always looking for an edge; I liked to smooth things over. They liked to take risks; well, I did, too, but not if those risks could land me in jail.

They became drug dealers; I was just a drug user. They made millions; I could barely afford new boots. They invested in Persian rugs, which would lie six deep on the floor; I dreamt of the day I could install wall-to-wall.

They were gamblers, willing to risk money or their own safety; the proudest week of my life was when I went to Vegas for a book conference and didn't put one nickel in the slot machines.

I wasn't like them.

◆ ◆ ◆

For eleven years, I helped Steve run his woodworking shop and sculpture studio. Steve was uncomfortable around money and had no idea how much he needed to get by, so I became the bookkeeper. I paid every bill that came in, and figured out how to hold off the creditors when there wasn't enough to go around. I was The Pencil's daughter, and Steve slept soundly, knowing that he never had to worry about money again. We made good friends, found a life that suited us. On vacation in Puerto Rico one year, we met a fabulous couple, Chris and Annie Flanders, who lived in Soho and had a weekend house in Wood-stock. Chris designed downtown lofts and Annie was the style editor of the *Soho Weekly News*. After we had been friends for a couple of years, Annie started the origi-nal *Details* magazine, which catered to a hip downtown crowd. I was infatuated with *Details*—although I had no interest in fashion or the club scene, I couldn't wait for it to arrive every month. It was an entree into a world where everyone was glib and smart, where ideas were important, where passion outweighed everything else. A few years later I had some plastic surgery—I had my breasts made smaller—and Annie asked me to write about it for *Details*. The piece was the first in a series called "Knifestyles of the Rich and Famous," and it became a huge sensation. Annie asked me if I wanted to write for the magazine on a regular basis and I jumped on it. I continued to contrib-ute to *Knifestyles* by helping other people tell their stories, and in 1987 I started writing a monthly book appreciation column called *Book 'Em*, bringing writers like Jane Smi-ley, Richard Ford, Ray Carver, and T. C. Boyle to a new community of readers. After a year or so I began to do celebrity interviews, and it turned out I was really good at it. I loved the research and was intimidated by no one. I started writing for other magazines, and within a few years I was flying around the world, watching movies for a living, having the time of my life. I went to Rome and split a fabulous lunch with Susan Sarandon; had a bout of hepatitis in an L.A. hotel room and writer/producer/director J. J. Abrams brought me chicken soup every night; joined Elizabeth Taylor and Larry Fortensky for a barbecue at Taylor's house.

Life was good.

THREE

Playing Poker with
My Dead Uncles

In 1990 I was sent to Los Angeles by *Details* to do a story about David Rabe's play *Hurlyburly*. Rabe was directing this play for the first time, with a cast that included Sean Penn, Danny Aiello, and Mare Winningham. I was supposed to have access to the entire cast, but from the minute I arrived, Penn wouldn't come anywhere near me. He was married to Madonna at the time and had a very contentious relationship with the press—the *New York Daily News* had recently called them "the most despicable couple on the planet." And as much as everyone around him tried to convince him that I was cool, Penn saw me as the enemy. One of the shows producers, Randy

Finch (*Miles from Home, Carolina Skeletons*), became my ally and smoothed things over between us.

A few months later I was back in Los Angeles, and was invited to see *Hurlyburly*'s last performance, and to go to the wrap party. In the time I had been away, Penn and Madonna had been in the papers nonstop—it was during that time that he was accused of trussing her to their bed and leaving the house. By closing night, they were no longer together and Penn was remarkably good-natured and chatty. He actually apologized for his bad behavior and invited me to come to Omaha, Nebraska, where he was going to direct his first film, *The Indian Runner.*

Randy and I kept in touch after my *Hurlyburly* story was printed. A few years later he approached me about writing a screenplay together. For three years we worked on a story about the circus. It was going to be a laugh-till-you-cry epic about a man who inherits his family's circus and hates every part of it, until, through the love of a sexy trapeze artist, he comes to realize how strong his roots are and falls back in love with what had captured him as a boy.

We did most of the research in Sarasota, Florida, winter home of Ringling Brothers. We put a small sign up in the sand at Crescent Beach that said: PLEASE TALK TO US ABOUT CIRCUS. Within days we had met Edith Wallenda, of the famous Flying Wallenda aerialist family, and had been to her home to see family photos and the low wire that was still set up in her backyard. We were introduced to Theo Zacchini, who claimed to be the first man to be shot out of a cannon. "I'm deaf now," he said, hobbling around his warehouse, where he still made carnival rides.

We tried to sell the script for close to two years, and although we had a few nibbles, nothing panned out. When we were ready to shelve it we were contacted by a small production company that wanted to pick up an option on the screenplay for a year. The money they were offering didn't cover the hotel rooms we had rented in Sarasota, but it gave us hope, and we signed the deal. We started outlining another screenplay immediately. Randy wanted us to write a film about two con men who rob a jewelry store and fall in love with one of their victims. We agreed that our film should star two women—okay, not just any two women, but Susan Sarandon and Michelle Pfeiffer in particular. We decided that one of the women should be a poker shark, and Randy sent me off to do the research.

In early 1995, I went to visit my cousin Keith in Fort Lauderdale so he could teach me to play poker. He played professionally in Vegas for a few years, and I wanted him to teach me what I'd need to know to make this character come to life. He dealt the cards and cooked, two things he does best, if you don't count selling drugs. Which we don't. Count anymore, I mean. He gave that up a long time ago. He's expansive in what he'll teach me about cards, a little stingier with the recipes. He's still upset about the balsamic vinegar.

It had happened a couple of years before, when he first got out of jail. The telephone rang at six. "You take a chicken breast," he said, not bothering with hello, "and you pound it really, really thin."

"Do I have to get a pen?" I'd asked, sitting up and knocking the newspapers to the floor.

"Nah, it's really easy." I could hear a pot being shaken, the sizzle of garlic hitting oil. I pictured the pile of parsley he always chops before every meal, which he sprinkles on everything he brings to the table, making all his dishes look like miniature Nordic villages. "Dip them in flour that you've mixed with black pepper. And use fresh-ground, I hate when you use the kind that's in the can."

I ignored him. He'd been bossing me around since I was six and he was seven, when he convinced me to go into the living room, where our parents and their friends, including the rabbi and his wife, were having a party. He wanted me to sing the song he had just taught me, and I did—I sang it with gusto. *I just got paid / And I want to get laid / Said Barnacle Bill the sailor.* I expected wild applause; instead, their mouths hung open. I took that as encouragement and started singing it again, until my mother steered me out of the room and took me back to Keith.

"You sauté the chicken really fast in olive oil and garlic," Keith continued on the phone, "and then sprinkle on balsamic vinegar. I just found out about it and it's really delicious—"

I cut him off. "Oh, I have some here. I love it."

Dead silence.

"What?" I asked, already feeling the spike of his anger.

"When did you find out about it?" he asked.

"Balsamic vinegar? A few years ago. You know that girl we like to watch on that cooking show? The one who stuck her hand all the way up the turkey that time? She gave a recipe for chicken sautéed with red and yellow peppers, topped with balsamic vinegar and sesame seeds. I use it all the time now."

He let out a long breath. "I've been out of jail for six days. I tasted balsamic vinegar for the first time exactly one hour ago. And I couldn't wait to get home and call you. I would never have kept balsamic vinegar a secret from you for years."

I could have reminded him that he'd been in jail, that he wouldn't have been able to taste it, that I didn't want to tease him. But that wouldn't have worked: he called from jail all the time. "You have a collect call from Keith, who's calling from a corrections institute," the operator would say, and he'd make me describe every taste, every new dish, every weird herb I'd eaten. "Arugula," he'd said the first time I'd told him about it, rolling the word around on his tongue. "Is it a flat leaf? Does it have a mustard taste? Is it bitter, like endive?" He wouldn't let up, until finally I drew it, or a bad likeness of it, and mailed it to him at Allenwood, making sure to use the right prisoner number (259712) so some poor guy who was waiting for news from his family wouldn't be brokenhearted when he got a picture of a lettuce that's wildly popular in Italy.

We breathed at each other for a minute, until I croaked out, "I'm sorry." I knew he was disgusted with me.

So now we're in his kitchen in Florida, and he's telling me about straights and flushes, but he refuses to divulge whether it's capoccolo or prosciutto that gives his lasagna such a zing. "Why should I tell you?" he taunts me, hiding a jar of red pepper flakes. I ignore him, and stare at "the list" I'd made up for myself.

It says:

ONE PAIR
TWO PAIRS
3-OF-A-KIND
STRAIGHT
FLUSH
FULL HOUSE
4-OF-A-KIND
STRAIGHT FLUSH

Keith hates the list and doesn't understand why I need it. "Because I can't remember what comes between three-of-a-kind and four-of-a-kind," I whine.

"You better remember, because those are the hands that are going to win you money." He lights a cigar and holds the match under the list. "You're smart," he says as it bursts into flames. "Just remember the fucking thing."

He deals out seven hands, but we only look at our own two. "The other five assholes'll stay in anyway," he assures me. "In a seven-card game, only stay in if you've got a high pair, three cards towards a straight, or three cards towards a flush. If not, fold and it hasn't cost you anything but your ante. And as soon as you see your hand going south, fold." As my father had told me, *If you don't have anything, get out.*

Keith deals out the rest of the cards, and while I pretend to listen to his advice, to my dead father's advice, I stay in when I shouldn't and wind up winning with a small straight. I am mighty pleased with myself.

"Show me your cards in the order you got them," Keith hisses angrily. I could lie, but he's like a truth-seeking missile and I don't dare. I show him the cards. He is appalled. "You should have folded after the third card," he says.

"C'mon, I won," I say, showing him my cards, showing him my tits, anything to make him laugh.

But poker is the one thing in his life that isn't a laughing matter. And it's the only thing he's ever been conservative about. Later I will watch him play—in Vegas, on a cruise, with friends in a low-stakes game. He's unbelievable. He kibitzes all the time, then counts cards while everyone else is busy laughing at his jokes. He folds so often that other players start to get nervous, thinking he knows something they don't. Actually, he does. He'll show his cards to the other players, which drives them nuts, whether they have him beat or not. He's a winner a lot more often than a loser.

"You know why?" he asks, baiting me. "Because I don't stay in with shit, hoping to pull a low straight." To prove this he makes me an offer: he'll give me fifty cents every time I stay in when I shouldn't—and I win the hand. In return, I only have to give him a quarter every time I stay in when I shouldn't—and I lose the hand. It seems like a great deal, but within four hours I'm down over twenty dollars.

"Get it?" he asks, pocketing the money and clearing away penne with roasted tomatoes. "Don't put them in the blender," he warns. "They're better when you crush them through your fingers." Then he sets out two little rame-kins of peach cobbler, the pastry forming perfect peaked caps. "At most, one in four hands is worth staying in," he says, turning serious. "That means that three-quarters of the time, you're not playing. Most people can't stand being out of the action that long, so they go in on hands they shouldn't. If you want to be a moron, that's the way you'll play, too. But if you want to win—and the only reason to play poker is to win—you'll listen to me. You'll fold most of the time. That's the first rule. There's no point in teaching you about money management, bluffing, pot odds, or anything else if you stay in with hands that aren't good. When you fold, watch the other players. Watch how they look when they have a good hand, watch how they look when they lose."

He leans over and wipes a crumb from my lip and without thinking flicks his tongue out to taste it. "Sometimes you have a good hand, maybe even a great hand, but you're pretty sure someone at the table has you beat. Fold. Don't get attached to your hand. You have good instincts, so trust them." *If you're second best, get out.* "And remember—don't whine, don't gloat. Just play your game, and keep the same attitude, however you're doing. This confuses people and they'll assume you're winning. And when they think you're winning, they'll make mistakes, or act like fools, and you will win."

◆ ◆ ◆

When we were kids, Keith was always the favorite. His parents didn't have as much money as the rest of the aunts and uncles—the Major worked at the post office—so our mothers and our aunts would indulge Keith in anything. They'd make sure he got the best chair when we all piled into the living room to watch television, or they baked a special loaf of challah that nobody else could touch, "in case he gets hungry later." They thought it was adorable when he started having sex, but didn't think it was quite so cute when they found out that we girls were fooling around, too.

We called him "the man with a plan." He knew that Frank's Shoe Store on the corner doubled as a place to buy stolen goods and often hung around there after school. When Broadway's wife, Eileen, stopped into Yogi's luncheonette for a chocolate egg cream and a hard pretzel one day and came out to find her new television missing from the backseat of her Caddy, it was Keith who went to Frank's and bought it back. "Only twenty bucks," he kept saying, as if it was such a deal. Broadway rewarded him with a tiny transistor radio, and it was only later that we realized that the radio was stolen, too.

Keith always had a scam going, whether it was taking wagers on playground basketball games, or hot goods. He would play poker in the schoolyard with the other fourteen-year-olds, but while they would come with their allowance, Keith would show up with two or three hundred dollars. They couldn't afford to stay in long enough to see whether he was bluffing, and he'd win all the big pots.

He was a basketball star at Van Buren but was flunking three subjects. While the cheerleaders stood around in their short skirts, chanting *Keith, Keith, he's our man, if he can't do it, no one can!* his mother begged me to tutor him in math. He'd come over after practice, all sweaty and excited, and I'd try to explain geometry while he tried to feel me up. I must have drawn that right angle a thousand times, but he'd just give me a stupid look and shrug. He needed real-life examples.

"When you're going to school," I said one day, barely concealing my annoyance, "you either go up Bell Boulevard and turn left on Union Turnpike, or you take the path through Alley Pond Park. Which one is shorter?"

"You can't drive through the park," he pointed out.

"Walking, you putz, not driving."

"Oh, then the park's shorter, definitely," he said.

"Right. Absolutely. Now, if you squared the distance of Bell and Union and added them up, they'd equal the square of Alley Pond. That means that the straight line is always shorter than the two sides of the right angle. That's the Pythagorean theorem."

He wasn't impressed. He'd make me deals: if I did his math homework, he'd pay for the tickets to see the Allman Brothers at the Fillmore East. If I'd write his essay on life in colonial America, he'd pick me up for school all fall. In my junior year, he turned me on to pot and pills—blue and red ones that he stole from Unc, acid that came on sugar cubes, some speed that made us both crazy. We wound up on the side of the Clearview Expressway one night, our nerves jangled, absolutely sure that the car, which was stalled, was going to blow up. We stood there, arguing, until he convinced me to get back in and try the ignition, promising me more drugs and a new *Sgt. Pepper* album. When the thunderous explosion that we were expecting failed to materialize, we celebrated by taking a couple of the Tuinals, which he persuaded me to snort. "It'll work quicker that way," he said. A minute later my nose started bleeding all over both of us. The next day he told my mother that he'd accidentally knocked me in the face with his elbow. "It's not your fault, sweetie," she said, brushing a stray hair from his forehead.

He didn't gloat when he got away with something—he just took more risks. He did everything all the way. When other people let their hair grow in the sixties, his was an Afro of Medusa-like proportions. He became a pirate, traveled the world, sent postcards from places we'd never heard of.

When he was in the money, everyone had a ball. For his twenty-fifth birthday, he flew fifty of us down to Austin for a private Grateful Dead show at a rodeo, handed over a sack of money when Steve's woodworking shop burned down, and gave each of the aunts ten thousand dollars.

He slept with women who were angular and bony. Scores of them. They let the hair in their armpits grow as long as his Afro. Then he fell for a woman who was so gorgeous that it felt good just to be in her presence. She was a natural beauty with a mass of golden hair. We assumed— incorrectly, it turned out—that she was a good person. She was macrobiotic and was pretty sure her shit didn't stink. At Thanksgiving she kept asking, "Tofu turkey sandwiches, anyone?" We all fell on the floor, laughing.

She wanted him to marry her, but he wouldn't. While the rest of us got married and divorced—and sometimes married and divorced again, and sometimes married and divorced from each other—not one woman could make him take a trip down the aisle. He left her right before he went to Alaska and bought a gold mine.

Then, about fifteen years ago, he called from Vegas to say he was bringing his new girlfriend to meet Steve and me. They arrived at two in the morning, and we woke up only long enough to notice she was wearing at least her share of makeup. The next morning I glanced outside at six a.m. and there she was: hair teased into a French twist, wearing twice as much makeup as the night before, eating a piece of chocolate cake, drinking a Coke, and smoking a cigarette. She had on a silk robe and three-inch mules with red feathers.

I woke Keith up. "Changing your type?" I asked. He scratched his hairy chest and yawned. "This is the one I'm gonna marry." Then he told me that the first time he saw her, in the poker room at Caesars Palace, he went over to her and her girlfriend and said, "Hello, ladies. Are you working tonight?" I looked at him, confused. "I thought they were prostitutes," he explained. He loved her all the more for looking like a hooker. And as if she didn't already look the part, her name was Barbie.

A year later, they flew ten of us to Lake Tahoe for their wedding, held at a drive-through chapel with an Elvis impersonator and his wife. My aunts went berserk—they could tell she was just after his money. Couldn't I see that? Couldn't everybody see that? But Keith had his bet down on the right woman: long after the money was gone (to lawyers), long after he'd gone to jail (even the lawyers couldn't prevent that), long after he was considered a good catch (a good catch? a drug dealer without a permanent address?), Barbie was still there. It was she who turned their lives around, settling with the IRS, getting a job in real estate, hoarding and scraping so that when he got out of jail they could really start fresh.

Now she's a poker dealer at the Seminole Indian reservation outside of Hollywood, Florida.

"Never think of folding as the booby prize," Keith tells me now. "Don't you remember how our fathers used to play?" He closes his eyes. "The Major was a good player," he says, talking about his own father. "Won a little each week, but couldn't bluff to save his life. Broadway couldn't stand to be out of the action, played seven out of eight hands. He won sometimes, sure, but lost big most other times. When you're playing poker, you pray to have someone like him at your table, because he's sure to make you a winner if you play tight. Cha Cha was a loose cannon, and you never knew if he was raising because he had a good hand or because he wanted you to fold. He was a big loser over the long haul, and the kind of guy you want in a game, although you probably wouldn't be able to bluff him out because he'd 'want to keep you honest.' Remember, you don't ever have to keep anyone honest—that's complete bullshit."

He takes a minute before he goes on. "Unc used to stay in too many hands, but he had something else going for him: he was lucky. And you cannot underestimate luck, especially when you're playing cards. Sammy B was a terrible player, but that didn't stop him from coming every week and dropping a bundle. He used to say, 'If I don't lose at poker, who will?' The Pencil...your dad, he was the best. They knew he wouldn't stay in with nothing, so they were leery of him when he was betting big. He was the best bluffer. He'd fold five out of six hands, then win one and bluff on the next three and they'd never be the wiser. It was like they were fish and he was reeling them in." *If you have the goods, make them pay.* "It's the same at every poker table you sit at. Once you type someone, you'll know how to play against them. It's that simple."

It's a lot to keep track of. And I still haven't memorized "the list."

FOUR

Wednesday-Night Poker

I need some real hands-on poker experience, so I ask my buddy Sal if he'd take me to his regular game. Sal is a stocky Italian, an ex–wild man who now plays golf as obsessively as he once pursued other habits. Sal tells me he'll have to ask the other guys first—"We've never played with a woman," he explained apologetically—but he reports back that they are so happy to have another body to fill an empty chair, they wouldn't care if I was a bisexual hermaphrodite with a stutter. "As long as you bring cash," Sal says cheerfully.

I spend that Wednesday afternoon repeating my mantra: straight, flush, full house. Straight, flush, full house. I consider writing it on my hand, like the crib sheets I used to make for high school tests, but ultimately I memorize it before I go out the door.

These guys have been playing together, with some additions and one death, for close to fifteen years: Michael, who owns a local restaurant, is tall and handsome, with piercing blue eyes and a patrician nose; Doc is a solidly built male nurse who lives over an hour away; Lefty is a New York City real estate agent who has a house in Woodstock and comes up on Wednesdays to play golf and poker; and Pete is a beefy ex-sheriff who barely glances my way. I sit down next to Michael, which turns out to be fortuitous, because he's the best player at the table and he's very generous with his knowledge. "Let me know if I do something stupid," I tell them, "because I'm just learning."

"Okay," Michael says softly. "It's dealer's choice, and the dealer antes for everybody. It's quarter, half, dollar, with no more than three raises. No check/raise. We pay five-dollar royalties for four-of-a-kind or a straight flush. You shuffle your own cards, and cut for the dealer in front of you. We use a red deck and a blue deck so there's no confusion. Any questions?"

Any questions? I haven't the slightest idea what he's talking about. I try to stop my hands from shaking and look at my cards. A pair of kings in the hole (the face-down cards). I can't even fold. The first time I throw a quarter on the table, this thought goes through my mind:

You're either a cheater or you're not, and this is probably the place it all comes out. I realize right then that I will never do anything at this table that I can't live with in the outside world.

That first night I make every conceivable mistake: I announce my straight before all the cards have been dealt, I accidentally turn up my hole cards, I open my hands while shuffling, something I haven't done since I was a kid, causing all fifty-two cards to career in different directions. Everyone just smiles at me.

Keith would be proud of me, though—I fold like crazy. It's not so much that I believe his wisdom, but because I don't know how to play the games they deal. Five-card stud, but you can buy another card at the end. High-low games, which I've never even heard about. Draw poker, but you need at least jacks to open and three-of-a-kind to win. "Jacks/trips," they call it. Seven-card stud games where you split the pot with whoever has the low spade among their hole cards.

"Please don't make me deal," I plead, my hands oddly uncomfortable with the cards, unsure of which game to choose. They agree to let me out of dealing.

"You shouldn't pass on your deal," Sal quietly scolds me later, when we're in the kitchen getting some chips and salsa. "You're the only one at this table who's looking to deal you a winner." I don't want to embarrass myself in front of him, so I force myself to deal when it's my turn again, picking whatever game the guy in front of me just dealt, the rules still straight in my head.

After a few hours of buying and selling chips, I realize that Kenny Rogers' advice about not counting your money when you're sitting at the table has a good rhythm but is complete nonsense. You have to count every hour or so to see where you stand.

"Always keep the same attitude . . . ," Keith had warned, and while it's a great philosophy, I'm not sure I can do it. I'm exhausted from shuffling, and counting chips, and rolling joints between hands—it's like another table rule. I feel like Lucy at the chocolate factory.

When I told my mother I was going to my first poker game, she gave me one piece of advice. "Never be a *whats-ittome*," she said.

"A what?" I asked, stumped.

"It's the idiot who never knows how much the bet is when it's their turn. The one who always says, 'What's it to me?' Keep track of the raises. Be ready with your money if you're staying in. Don't screw up the flow of the game."

This turns out to be great advice. Even though I feel like I'm playing underwater, I try not to slow up the game, and everyone notices and appreciates it.

My mother started playing poker during the Depression, when Tillie's mother ran an illegal game in her Bronx apartment. My mother and Tillie were in charge of food for the players—my mother told me about the platters of brisket and potatoes, carmelized onions and carrots, plates of fresh fruit they would serve. My mother would walk around and fill the men's cups with hot tea; Tillie would pour shots of whiskey. Tillie's mother took a dollar or so out of each pot, and gave my mother and Tillie a small cut. But when one of the men wasn't there, my mother would sit in and play. She told me that for the first year she lost every single week, money that Tillie's mother would stuff in her pocketbook later that night. My mother hated taking that money, because times were so tight for everyone. So she started paying attention, asking questions, and began holding her own. Eventually she became a good and skilled player. "The men hated playing with me," she told me with a smile.

Now I'm sitting at a poker table with five men, asking a million questions, learning about etiquette and rules, figuring my movie character would have this information down cold. And these fine points seem more important than whether I win or lose.

I end the night up four dollars, not through any skill but because of some good luck and a big hand even a blind man could have won. When they ask me to come back the next week, I feel like I've been asked to the prom.

The next morning, Sal's wife, Karen, comes over to see if I had fun. "It was great," I tell her. "But Lefty's cheating."

The words are out of my mouth before they have fully formed in my brain. Karen winces. Sal and Lefty grew up together in Baltimore and used to spend a lot of time golfing, until they were searching the rough for Lefty's ball one day and Sal saw him take another out of his pocket, drop it, and say that it was the first ball. Sal stopped playing with him after that. When Karen asks me *how* Lefty is cheating, I admit that I'm not sure. "There's just something he's doing that's not right," I say. "He talks too much when he's dealing, moves his hands around too much. It's like he's about to pull a rabbit out of his shirt. But maybe I'm wrong. Don't tell Sal yet."

When Keith calls to see how I did, I go over the best and the worst hands of the night. I tell him about Michael—about how he lets me look at his cards when I'm not in a hand, about how patient he is with me. I describe a hand that started out well but which I eventually lost. "But it was okay," I say, "because Sal and Michael split the pot . . ."

"Stop playing if you want them to win," Keith hisses.

I chatter on for a minute or so until I realize he's hung up on me.

I wander over to the couch and pick up a deck of cards. I deal out six hands, playing all the games I learned last night, just to see which hand would win if we all stayed until the end. I deal again and again, until Steve calls to tell me he's on the way home. I look up and realize that the sun has set. The next day I don't even bother getting dressed. I sit on the couch in my bathrobe, dealing the cards out endlessly. I keep score for myself: Should I have stayed in or not with my opening cards? Would they have been the winner? What Keith told me seems solid—a bad opening rarely turns into a winner. I spend most of that week playing poker by myself.

When I go to the next game I feel as if I know a little more. Every time I have something good, though, Lefty or Doc raise me and I believe they have something better. I fold seven times when I would have won, and start to feel humiliated.

"Ante up," Michael keeps reminding me. "Cut the cards toward the dealer," he says. Michael and I get a lot of time to talk, because we both fold more often than the others. Lefty, Doc, and Pete are in almost every hand. "A buck," one of them will say. "And a buck," the next one will shout. "And another buck," the third will taunt. "The chickens are out of the barn," Michael says, and it takes me a minute to understand. Buck, buck, buck.

When there's an argument about what to do when the dealer inadvertently turns over a card out of order, everyone bellows their opinions. "At least nobody here has a gun," I say innocently. Sal, Michael, and Lefty laugh, but neither Doc nor Pete can meet my eyes. It does not make me feel good to realize that a third of the people in this room are armed.

I am completely thrown by their terminology: they remark how they had "ladies," or "a pair of cowboys," or "three bullets," and the others mutter in acknowledgment. I ask Michael what the hell they're talking about, and he explains that it's shorthand for queens, kings, and aces. "Are you betting on the come stain?" they ask each other, half seriously. That one I figure out for myself; it means the hand is a wet dream, not yet a winner, though it might be with the right card. When my pair of aces is beat by two small pairs, Michael looks at my cards and says, "Hmmm, aces and spaces."

There is an energy at this table that I'm not used to. For years I played mah-jongg with my girlfriends, who like to mine each nuance for its intrinsic meaning. They would constantly interrupt the game to see how you were, how you felt, what you're thinking, how you think you might feel. Mah-jongg was the excuse—gossip and friendship were the real reason we were there. But the only thing these guys talk about is poker and golf. I'm not sure who's married, who has kids, what they do for a living. They laugh and make jokes, but there is no intimate talk. I find it refreshing.

I keep my eye on Lefty, but it's hard to tell what he's doing. When I notice him not throwing the right amount into the pot, I mildly suggest that he owes another dollar. He stares right through me. "No, I don't," he says easily.

Over the next few weeks I ask Michael some of the questions that have been bothering me: in a draw game, where all your cards are dealt to you facedown, would I be better off drawing two cards to the three spades I have, or to keep a nine, ten, queen, and king, hoping to pull a jack?

"When should you draw inside to a straight?" he asks rhetorically. "Never, never, and never."

Does he think I should bet my three-of-a-kind the minute I get it, or bet slowly so I can wind up with a bigger pot?

"If they're little, bet them quickly," he says. "But if they're big"—he moves his mouth in right next to my ear—"bet them slowly. Very, very slowly." I turn away so he won't see that my face has turned crimson.

I am besotted with Michael, with everything about him. The way he touches my shoulder when he speaks, the way he lowers his voice so I have to lean in closer to hear him, the way his fingers caress the cards, as if they were his lovers and shuffling was just slow, languid foreplay.

His Adam's apple protrudes, his fingers are long and thick. I can't help but wonder...but then I remember Frankie Boyd, a boy I had a crush on in college. Frankie had fingers that looked like bursting sausages, and a penis that resembled a shriveled mushroom. I try to push the thought out of my mind.

In the old days, I would have moved things along with Michael. I would have let my thigh linger against his under the table, I would have reached over and wiped an imaginary crumb off his mouth. I remember a guy I did that to in a bar in Miami Beach: my finger had pushed at the fleshy part of his lower lip, and before I could snatch it back he had engulfed it in his mouth. I could feel tongue, and teeth. I spent the night with him at his sleazy motel, and most of the next day, but I never did get his name. On my list, I referred to him as "the blond guy in the Aztec Motel with the great cowboy boots." He had made me come by resting the toe of his boot against my crotch and tapping out Willie Nelson's "To All the Girls I've Loved Before."

In the old days, I would have taken a Quaalude and pushed Michael against a wall. I would have licked places on his body that he didn't even know existed, had him begging me not to stop.

But I'm not like that anymore. And the old days are just that—old. These days a little flirting never hurts. Steve and I have never felt threatened by each other's flirtations, and in fact, he knows how wild I am about Michael because I never stop talking about him.

In my most lucid moments I can see that Michael isn't

even coming on to me; he's just being polite and explaining the finer points of poker to a newcomer.

So I put those thoughts out of my mind and let Michael be my teacher. His mind works the same way mine does; he understands numbers, and he explains everything in terms of percentages and probabilities. Often, when we are debating about why you are more likely to make one hand over another, no one else at the table seems to understand, or care, what we're talking about.

Sal and I talk poker, too, but it's different—Sal is very competitive by nature and doesn't want to give me too much information. It's not that he holds back, exactly, but he's a bit closefisted with his advice. Sometimes he will tell me that I did something silly, or point out that I should have raised more on a certain hand—but if I ask him, "Do you think you should bet heavily when you have two pairs?" he will just shrug. If I push the point, he'll say he doesn't know, although he's a good player and usually wins. I stop asking.

After each hand, we have what Michael calls "Kiner's Corner," after Ralph Kiner, the great baseball player and sports announcer, who would dissect every play of the game on his postgame show. Here everyone talks about what they presume you were thinking, why you raised, why you should have folded. I notice that Michael very rarely participates in these conversations. I watch him closely and realize that he doesn't want to give away any information, and that this is smart, because every time you tell your opponents something, they can use it against you later. But I listen. Oh, I listen, and I learn so much about all the players. And sure enough, week after week I start to do better and better.

I call Keith and tell him that I get it—Sal is like Unc, a solid player who is also very lucky; Lefty is our Broadway, a compulsive gambler who doesn't care what he's betting on; Doc is Cha Cha reincarnated—who could tell if he had a good hand or if he was trying to bluff you out? And Michael was like The Pencil, the strong, silent type who won consistently.

"And you?" Keith asks. "Which one are you?"

I don't know yet.

I spend the next week on the couch, and the week after that. When editors call to offer stories, I explain that I'm too busy—I'm doing research for a film. I actually use the word *film*, which sounds so much more important than *movie*.

When Randy calls to ask how the research is going, I tell him about the past Wednesday's game. He is flummoxed and keeps pushing me to start writing.

Winter turns to spring, spring to summer. When Steve wants to meet for lunch, I tell him, maybe tomorrow. When he wants to go to the movies, I say, no, we can rent it in a few months. My garden is neglected, the fabric on my couch starts to wear thin, friends get annoyed that I rarely return their calls. But I am in a poker frenzy, and each week I do a little better. Does it strike me as odd that I'm turning down four- and five-thousand-dollar assignments so I can possibly win eighty-five bucks on Wednesday? No, it doesn't strike me as odd at all. In fact, it seems perfect. Absolutely perfect.

FIVE

Playing Like a Girl

Still there is so much I don't know. I spend another few months on the couch playing poker, days sliding into night, rarely wondering what I'm doing. Randy keeps telling me to forget the research and start writing the screenplay, and my editors are unable to grasp why I'm not jumping at the opportunity to interview fabulous movie stars. But something has taken hold of me, and I haven't felt this exhilarated in years.

The week is neatly divided: on Wednesdays I am in a frenzy, trying to deal out dozens of hands of the games I know we will play that night. Thursdays are bad, because I can only go over what I did wrong. Poker players rarely think of the things they did right—that's what they expect from themselves. Fridays and Saturdays are the worst, because the next game is so far away, so I try to teach myself new games, figuring I can use any edge I can get. These guys have been playing poker for years, have seen thousands of hands. I'm only trying to catch up. On Sundays I go cold turkey—no poker at all so I can have some real time with Steve. Our relationship has never been clingy and needy, and we've both been free to pursue the things we love. Steve works in wood and metal, but his real love is cars from the fifties, and he has become well known for mixing those mediums into both usable furniture and monumental outdoor pieces. He works till eight or nine o'clock most nights, and I'm happy to wait and have dinner with him whatever time he comes home. But he's starting to cringe whenever he hears the sound of shuffling cards, and I could use the break myself.

By Monday I'm back on the couch, playing a particular game for eight or nine hours, the patterns imprinting on my brain, my mood considerably brighter. If someone has introduced a new game, I'll spend a day just playing that; it's amazing what you can learn by sheer repetition. By Tuesday my hands are nearly crippled from shuffling the cards. "Carpal tunnel," I tell people, letting them believe that writing is wreaking havoc on my body. Before Sal picks me up to go to the game on Wednesday night, I soak my hands in ice water.

Each week I learn something new. There are fifty-two

cards in the deck, but for practical purposes I pretend that there are fifty, making the chance of getting any particular card two percent, the chance of getting a card of a particular suit twenty-five percent. I deal out the hands and figure out the chances of each one winning. I can feel my father grinning down at me with delight.

After I've been playing for a little less than a year, I get my first real lesson in poker. We're playing a high/low game. These pots tend to be larger, because they will be split by two people—the person with the high (best) hand and the person with the low (worst) hand. Michael has explained to me that Ace-2-3-4-6 is the best possible low hand, because Ace-2-3-4-5 would be a straight, and that doesn't count for a low. I have a perfect low, Ace-2-3-4-6. Sal and Lefty go high, Doc and I go low. I know I have him beat, and I know that he's been losing all night, so I turn to him and say, "Doc, get out, I have the nuts [the best hand]." Sal smiles at me and Michael winks, but the look on Doc's face is quite different. He throws his cards down on the table and looks at me with loathing. I can hear the word escape his mouth. *Pussy.* He thinks I'm weak for letting him off the hook! That look totally confuses me—am I playing poker like a girl, for crissakes? And if I am, is that necessarily bad? I am so thrown that I barely know what's going on for the rest of the night, but I end up forty-five dollars ahead, which feels like a windfall.

I call Keith and ask him if women make good poker players. He reminds me of how, when we were kids, I always let him win at cards or board games. And the punishment for losing was always having my knuckles slammed with a deck of cards. "You would sit there until your hands were shredded and bleeding," Keith reminds me, "always on the edge of crying. You were so much smarter than me," he says unabashedly. "There's no way you couldn't have beat me. But you held back, you . . . well, you played like a girl. Poker is different. It's like warfare. You have to treat each hand like a skirmish, the whole night as the battle. If you can't see it that way, stop playing now, because you'll get killed." He points out that very few of the top poker players in the world are women. "It's because they can't go for the jugular."

Can *I*? I think of the women's softball league I helped organize in my town twenty years ago. At first there were only fifteen of us—we would play seven-man teams with a roving hitter. Within two years we had enough players for six teams. Men started showing up to cheer us on—it was the seventies, and none of the women wore bras. "This is the best show in town," one of the men confided in me. We started getting better and better, the level of play going up a notch every week. But then the men wanted to be coaches; within a year, the level of play was excellent, but morale was in the cellar. We finally got rid of the coaches and literally forced ourselves to play more competitively. I remember a game where our shortstop bobbled a ball. "Pick it up," I screamed at her from second base. When I ran toward her, I realized the ball had hit her square in the eye, which was now turning a deep shade of red. I got to her, and she reached her hand out, expecting me to help her up, I think. I fumbled under her leg, grabbed the ball, and threw it to the third baseman, who tagged the runner out. All the men congratulated me after our win, telling me how tight our team was, but I still recall the shock that rippled through the shortstop's body when she realized that I didn't care about her injury, only the outcome of the game. What the men praised me for embarrasses me still.

I spend the next few weeks watching myself at the game, analyzing when I should go for blood. What I see is that if it's Sal I'm up against, I don't go the extra bit to milk him of all the money I should. We spend three or four nights a week together—is this game worth making our friendship uncomfortable? For me the answer is no, but Sal seems happy to take another dollar or two from me when he can.

With Michael it's the same. He gives me advice all night, tells me after a hand whether he thinks I played it right or wrong, explains what the chances are of getting a card at any junction in the game. But if it's just the two of us left at the showdown, he raises and gets as much money as he can. And I don't think less of him for it.

All my life I've been programmed to please the men around me, to make them feel comfortable and not threatened. At the poker table I am likely to shrug off that last dollar or two, not wanting to push these men to the wall. Yes, I want to win, but more than that, I want them to like me. I realize that those two things might not be compatible, but this pleasing thing is deeply ingrained.

My girlfriends have often remarked that I think like a man—and they do not say this kindly. Men have always been comfortable with me; I can talk sports, drink them under the table, and flirt like crazy without letting them believe that I'm going to sleep with them. I like to do the things men like to do, but I never think of myself as one of the boys. And I don't think the men do, either.

And yet I can't help but notice that the men at this table treat me differently than they do each other. When they get beat by each other they say things like, "How the fuck did you get a hand like that?" They call each other "dick" and "asshole." But when Michael deals me a pair of queens, he smiles and says, "The queen has two queens." When I win with a totally hidden full house, Sal laughingly says, "The fleet is pulling in at Martha's." I realize that being a woman might have its advantages at the poker table . . . that it's great to be a girl as long as you don't act like one.

Because I'm new at this, they want to help me. They just

laugh when I do something stupid, start to tell me stories about their lives, generally treat me with respect and humor.

My mother comes for a visit and I take her to the game. The guys are very deferential to her, this tiny, bossy, Jewish General, until she wins five pots in a row. Then they start to treat her like a poker player. That only makes her play better. She makes fun of us for the silly games we play, and the amount of pot smoke in the room, but she never loses her focus and wins close to a hundred dollars. Afterward, we sit up till two in the morning, going over every hand. She gives me her read on the players, and tells me that she is proud of how well I did. My feet feel like they'll never hit the ground again.

One night, when Doc is raising and raising in a hand I know I will win, I ask him where he learned to play poker. I expect something glib, but he surprises me. "In Vietnam," he says. "I was a medic. You'd go into the bush for five weeks, and then they'd airlift you out, give you your pay, which looked like this huge pile of money. We'd get ten days until we went back in, and all we did was sit around and play poker—seven guys who were absolutely sure that the next time they went into the jungle they weren't coming out alive." And right then I understand how to play against him. In the future, when he raises me and I begin to get scared, thinking his hand might beat mine, I calm down by telling myself, "It's jungle time." He will never know how much he gave away by telling me that story, because once you know what motivates someone, you can get into their head and figure out when to stay or when to fold against them. And with Doc, I understood that he played poker as if he had nothing to lose.

Another night, when everyone else is busy, Pete leans over and says, "What do six niggers and six dykes have in common?" He says it low enough so I am the only one who hears it, and before I can react he answers his own question. "That's a dozen people who don't do dick!" He almost falls off his chair, laughing.

I start sputtering. I hate his guts, and spend the rest of the night trying to beat him. I don't need Keith to tell me what a bad idea this is, but I am so enraged that I just go on tilt. I lose twenty-five dollars. Pete wins forty. I think I might just grab his gun and shoot him.

The next week I come to the game ready to tell Pete what a racist, juvenile jerk he is, but he doesn't show up. "What'd you do to Pete?" the guys kid me, because obviously my reactions to him weren't as inscrutable as I'd imagined. Pete doesn't come the next week, or the one after that. Eventually I call a friend of mine, a sixties-hippie-type named Robert who once invented a pipe that sucked all the THC out of marijuana without any smoke, getting you more stoned than you'd imagine on even the most mediocre pot, and ask him if he'd like to play. He starts coming regularly, sometimes bringing other friends with him.

I call Keith every Thursday morning and go over certain hands with him. "Remember," he tells me one day, "a good player is always looking for a way to fold. A bad player's always looking for a way to stay in." The list of things Keith wants me to remember is longer than my arm.

I watch Lefty like a hawk, and while I see him short the pot at least once an hour, I'm not sure what to do. I try to embarrass him, telling him dozens of times a night that I think he owes a little more money. But he just gives me a shrug and ignores me. Then I see him do something that I know spells trouble. When a player runs out of chips in the middle of a hand, instead of stopping the game to buy more chips, they let him do what's called "drawing light." This means that for every dollar you're supposed to be putting in the pot, you pull a dollar toward yourself, building a little pile in front of you. Those are your "lights," and at the end of that hand, you're supposed to put all those chips back in the pot, plus another stack of an equal amount. When I had told Keith that drawing light was okay at this game, he said, "Bad idea. It's very hard to keep track of it. Make them change that rule."

There are guys who will stop the game to buy chips rather than draw light. There are others, myself included, who will make sure before a hand begins that they'll have enough chips for the hand. But Lefty will often start a hand with only a few dollars in front of him, and he's always drawing light. I start watching his pile of lights, and see that after he draws light for a card or two, he'll start throwing in those chips as if they belong to him. I tell the guys that I think we should stop drawing light, because it slows the game down. Lefty, of course, thinks that's a stupid idea, but the other guys agree, and we make it the rule that you have to buy chips before the hand starts or when you run out during a hand. One less thing to watch.

On the way home that night I finally tell Sal my suspicions about Lefty. He looks like I've punched him in the gut. "I don't know why I'm surprised," he says sadly. "I'll start watching him."

Lefty is the hardest person in the game to figure out. He stays in almost every hand, only folding when he's sure he's beat. He's aggressive and won't let you buy a card cheaply. If he does fold, he'll try to draw someone who's folded into a side bet with him; he just likes the action. When he wins, he talks about himself in the third person. "Lucky Lefty won a big pot," he'll say, as if he's an announcer on the radio.

"Slow-fuck him," Keith says when I explain his pattern. "For a couple of weeks, only stay in with a good hand against him. No, only stay in if you have a monster hand. But act scared. Let him be the one who's making all the bets, all the raises, let him be the one who thinks he's going to win. And when you turn over your winning hand, act surprised. You'll see, he'll start assuming you have a good hand even when you don't."

Sure enough, he's right. Every win I take from Lucky Lefty makes me feel elated. His smile gets a little tighter every time it happens. Plus, Sal and I are constantly telling him he's not throwing the right amount into the pot. He ignores Sal just as he's been ignoring me, but I can see that he's unnerved. I want to beat Lefty, but I don't want to go on tilt, doing stupid things that will make it easier for him to beat me. I try not to let him goad me, try not to listen to his stories or his bullshit.

Sal is my friend, Michael is my teacher; does this make me play differently against them? I watch myself and notice that it does. It's almost like I don't want to overstep some boundary that I have set up for myself, and I don't want them to think that I'm a bitch. But they don't seem to share my concern, and never even blink if they beat me. Many times I utter the word *sorry* when I beat them, and I can see their eyes glaze over. Apparently, there are no *sorry*s in poker. Each week I force myself to stop apologizing for doing well, and am surprised that no one seems to think less of me for it. Just the opposite, in fact.

I start not to care if I'm up against the guys I like, or the guy I don't.

A few months later, when I have a hand I know will win

and Michael is the only other person still in the game, I raise him again and again, making sure to squeeze every last quarter out of him. When I turn over my hand, a well-hidden full house, Michael looks me right in the eye. "You cunt," he hisses, and I can feel the other guys sucking in their breath. They look away in embarrassment. But I see the smirk on Michael's face spreading like red wine on a white tablecloth. His hand snakes under the table and he squeezes my leg. He is so proud of me—his student has finally learned her lesson.

SIX

My Poker Face

When I was seven I came into the kitchen, where my mother and Aunt Tillie were cutting onions for a pot roast dinner. I was carrying my wooden recorder, as I did most everywhere. I couldn't read music but could duplicate anything by ear, and that spring I had taught myself all the patriotic songs our class would play at the Flag Day assembly: "As the Caissons Go Rolling Along," "Battle Hymn of the Republic," "When Johnny Comes Marching Home Again." I had visions of myself as a soloist.

I had just spent the day with Barry Kaminsky, the boy to whom I was devoted. Barry was pudgy, slightly cross-eyed, had a lisp and a stammer, and was prone to punching when talking might be more effective. He was also very funny, was a great dresser, and always knew what skirt of mine would look best with which blouse, and taught me to kiss, which we would do for hours in the stairwell of my building. He was my best friend, and I had bruises all over my body from defending him against the other kids to prove it.

"So Barry and I made up this song on the recorder, wanna hear it?" My mother and Tillie nodded through their onion tears. I sucked on the end of the recorder until it felt soft in my mouth, the wood already waterlogged from practicing all day. I played the song, a sad, lamenting kind of tune that to this day makes me want to cry and eat a Hostess cupcake simultaneously.

"Pretty," said my mother, although we all knew she was tone deaf.

"What's it mean?" asked Tillie, ever the literalist.

I could have said that it meant nothing, that Barry and I just liked the way the notes sounded, one after the other. But a story was what they wanted, and a story was what I gave them.

"I had this dream that I was flying above Barry's house . . ." I looked up to see if they knew I was lying, and what I saw was this: they knew, and they wanted me to go on anyway.

"I grabbed his hand and we took off together. I took him to the place where I am the princess, and I made him the prince. We had lots of subjects—you know, people who did what we wanted them to. But we treated them good, we only made them do things they would do anyway." I walked over and dipped my finger in the pot, and licked off the sauce.

"Anyway, there was an old woman there. She was really nice. She made me a white cotton dress and then she cooked the best potato pancakes . . ." I looked up to see a quick pang of irritation cross Tillie's eyes; *she* made the best potato pancakes and we all knew it.

But I went on without apology. "We covered them with sour cream *and* applesauce, and nobody said we were gonna throw up. There's no vomiting where we were. The flying made us feel great, but then Barry's mother said he had to be home before dark, and he felt very sad. This is the song we came up with."

"Play it again," my mother said, and I did, happily, because I was worried that they'd make me describe flying, or ask if the applesauce was lumpy or smooth. When I was done, Tillie came right over to me, stinking of onions, and put her hand on the recorder.

"The next time," she said, "make the dress velvet . . ."

"Red velvet," my mother added, nodding her head to make her point.

"Good," said Tillie, as if she and my mother owned this story. "And don't make Barry the prince. Things will work out better that way, believe me."

They went back to their onions and I played that song again and again, until they were humming along.

Later that night, when we had mopped up every drop of pot roast gravy, my mother and Tillie told my father and Unc about my beautiful song and the great story that went with it. I was so happy and proud.

"Barry's making me a dollhouse!" I said out of nowhere.

They all looked my way. "I didn't know Barry knew how to build things," my father said.

"Yeah, he does. He and his father made a whole swing set for their backyard."

Now I had stepped over the line—they must have known that the Kaminskys' backyard was no bigger than our bathroom; surely they knew that Mr. Kaminsky was a skinny, unhappy man who smoked cigarettes in front of his house long after the kids had gone to bed and never spent any time with them.

But no one challenged me, so I went on. "It's going to have five bedrooms, the dollhouse, and it's going to have wood on the outside and real carpeting on the stairs. The kitchen is going to be so huge that my whole doll family could live in there. There's gonna be a grand piano and two televisions in the living room so no one has to share. It's gonna be great."

"Is that the truth?" my mother asked, looking a little concerned.

"Truth, schmooth," Tillie said before I could admit what a liar I was. "It's a good story."

Later on, after my father died, I got my Ph.D. in lying. If I was going to a friend's, I would tell my mother I was going to the library. If I stayed late at school, I would tell her that I had been to the movies, making up whole plots of films I knew she'd never see. The lies made me feel powerful, proved that I had a life that was all my own. The lies made me hate myself, pointed out how truly alone I was in the world.

The summer after my father died I went away to camp in the Catskill Mountains. I wrote to all my friends about my new boyfriend, Ira Silverman. Ira lived in our neighborhood and went to a bungalow colony right down the road from my camp. I didn't see Ira once that summer. But in my letters, Ira and I were swimming in isolated ponds, picking blueberries by the gallon, making out in his bedroom till our lips were bruised and chapped.

In September I went bowling with my friends, and who should walk in but Ira. My first thought was that I was happy to see him, although we had never had much of a relationship. But then I realized this was a setup; my girlfriends had asked him to come to confront me about what a fraud I was. I started shaking and they stood there with their arms crossed over their chests, expecting me to melt and die and admit the truth. I dug in my heels, kept talking to Ira as if he was the liar, begging him to remember things the way I had painted them. I saw in his eyes a mixture of pity and fear, and I fled.

Hours later, when I came home, looking as if I had been beaten, my mother was waiting at the door with a wet washcloth, having heard the story from my friend Paula's mother. I sputtered and cried, the snot bubbles exploding from my nose, as she rocked me and crooned that it was okay, that she loved me, that I'd be all right.

I stopped lying that day.

But at the poker table, it's acceptable, even encouraged. And lying is what makes the difference between winning and losing. After all, the odds are that we'll all get dealt the same amount of good or bad hands on any given night. It's the ability to win with hands that aren't really winners that brings the piles of chips in your direction. And, of course, luck.

At the game I find it hard to imagine that someone is bluffing; I just figure they have better cards than me. Afterward, I'll wonder if I was beat out by a real winner or a bluff, but how can I tell? On more than one occasion on the way home I'll ask Sal if he bluffed me out of a particular hand. But he's a little reluctant to tell me something that I will surely use against him in the future.

Keith's advice is that the best time to bluff is when you're on a roll. "Gamblers believe in streaks. They pray for them, in fact. More than that, they're praying that another player won't get on a lucky one. When you've won a couple of hands in a row, they think you're hot, and they're apprehensive about betting against you. That's the time to bluff—if you have cards that look like they might be winners."

The next week I try out his theory. At one point I win four in a row, all good, solid hands that couldn't be beat. My next hand is a sure loser, but I bet it as if it's just another in a string of great ones, and everyone folds in fear. Of course I get cocky, and I try bluffing the next pot as well. But Sal has three queens, and there's no way he's folding. Instead of just throwing my cards away and admitting defeat, I stay till the end and lose another five dollars. A few more times that night I try it again, but I get goosed out of the hands when nobody believes that I have the winner.

Sal and Michael are the easiest to bluff, because they're the best players and do not want to stay till the end only to find out that they're second best. This is exactly what Keith is talking about. I would have thought it was the other way around, that weak players would fold when you act strong. But as usual he's right.

Doc often can't be bluffed out, because he's staying till the end whether he has a good hand or not. It's both the *jungle* thing, and the *I'm gonna just keep you honest* nonsense. I know if it's just me and him, I better have something or I'll lose. Robert tries to read me, often stopping the game to stare into my eyes. I wonder what kind of things I'm revealing to him, because half the time he reads me correctly. Lefty's just plain nuts, a big bluffer himself, and, it turns out, easily bluffed, because more than anything he does not like to lose. Reading the people I'm playing against becomes as important as reading my own cards. I start to get a little better at it, but something's still missing.

So I go to the true source—my mother. Her advice is startling. "You blush when you lie—remember when you told me that story years ago about how you were sleeping at Lynn Kramer's but I knew you were lying because Lynn's mother called to tell me that Lynn was supposed to be sleeping at our house?"

I was dumbfounded, could not remember the incident

or Lynn Kramer. But my mother, at eighty-five, remembered every meal she ate, every conversation she had, the names of anyone who ever passed through her life. I believe her, and feel the disgrace of it.

"You were so red, you looked like a tomato," she continued. "So I picture you at the poker table, blushing like a schoolgirl if you try to bluff. But maybe you could start blushing regularly, especially when you're not bluffing, so they can't tell when you're lying. You'd have to imagine something that embarrasses you . . ." She went on, but I was already there—all those things I thought about Michael brought the blood to my face anyway.

The next week at poker I try the new blushing method. When I have a winning hand, I make myself blush. I catch their eyes, one by one, and make sure they see it before I turn over my winning hand. I do it all night, never once even trying to bluff, thinking filthy thoughts. Sal even remarks on it—"Either you've got the best hand you've ever had, or the worst," he says sweetly—but the others just take it in stride.

One night, when I have what they call great "scare cards," cards that look like they're winners, I start betting as if I have the other cards that go with them, which I don't. I start thinking about running my tongue over Michael's lower lip and feel myself turning red. I look up and smile. Everyone folds.

Now I'm watching the cards, trying to keep up, turning red by choice, and watching Lefty. No wonder I can't work on that screenplay.

Sal and I coerce Karen and Steve into learning poker—neither is particularly astute with numbers and both hate gambling, but they agree. We write the what-beats-what list on the back of a paper plate. Then we recruit another couple, two women, who come for dinner a few nights a week and like playing. Then a friend's son asks if I can teach him. He starts bringing other kids over, and we have these great pizza extravaganzas while we play. The boys are only twelve years old, but they're clever and learn quickly. Since poker doesn't work if you're not playing for money, we develop a system that requires everyone to put up the same amount of money. We decide that three dollars is a good sum, and at the end of the night, the people with the most chips will split the cash. The boys ask millions of questions about every aspect of poker, and these talks help me understand a lot more, as well. Then my godkids, who are six and seven years old, start playing with us, too. Their hands are almost too small to hold the cards, but they like playing so much that they figure out ways not to drop them. They bring three dollars each, and don't cry when they lose. There are nights when there are twelve people crowding around the dining table, kids and adults alike, passing that paper plate around and trying to win a dime or a dollar—it hardly matters.

As much as I love playing with the kids and with Steve and Sal and Karen, it's Wednesday nights that I live for. There's something about winning against those guys that makes me feel really accomplished.

Because I am looking at poker hands so often, I am usually the first one to read someone else's hand correctly at the game. Sal might say, "I have two pair," but when I look, I see that he really has a full house. Or Lefty might say that he has a flush, but I'll see that he only has four hearts and three diamonds. It gets to be a joke, that the least experienced player is the one with the quickest eye.

The guys who are the best at the table—Michael and Sal—rarely show their feelings. Sometimes on the way home Sal will tell me how angry he is about something that happened, but no one at the table would have known. Michael is the same. He is even-tempered and funny. But sometimes he gets very quiet. Whenever this happens, everyone at the table starts getting nervous. He is the rock of this group, and although he seems unaware of his power, he is a strong presence that everyone looks to.

My mother says I should watch myself when I know

I have the winning hand—do I lean in and throw my chips more aggressively? Do I pick up extra chips when I know I will be betting heavily? Do I tap my foot like a drummer on speed because I want the action to speed up? Yes, I do all these things. It's as if she's been in the room with us.

"How'd you know?" I ask.

"Those are the kinds of things all new players do," she says. "The minute you can hold your chips the same no matter what your hand, or keep your voice steady when you know you're the winner, that's when you'll be a good player."

This is something I can't teach myself on the couch.

The more I play with other people, the more I learn to keep my feelings to myself. If I lose a hand, I will not call the other player an idiot, will not throw my cards down in disgust, even if that's the way I feel. I train myself to just sit still, to smile, to act the same, win or lose. A Buddhist friend of mine calls it "being neutral."

"Always maintain the same attitude," Keith had urged me, and I start to see the logic. The minute you act pissed off you give the other player an advantage. And every advantage you give your opponent makes it harder to win.

I know I have perfected my poker face when I am sitting with an ace-high flush and slow-betting it. Doc says, "Honey, get out. I have you beat." The others laugh, but I shrug like a little girl and raise. He raises back. I re-raise. And when I turn over my cards, nobody says a word. I have finally stunned them into silence.

SEVEN

The Cruise

Keith and Barbie call with an intriguing offer: Barbie has been asked to deal poker on a five-night cruise to the Bahamas, and since she has to stay in a room with two of the other dealers, Keith wants me to come along and share a room with him. "It's on me," he keeps saying. Sun, swimming, and nonstop poker—all right, twist my arm. They send me photos of what appears to be a huge stateroom. HUGE! And a plane ticket to Fort Lauderdale.

Keith and I talk daily for the month before we leave. He's been on poker cruises before and wants me to understand that there will be higher-stakes games than I'm used to, and that some of the players will be really good.

"They'll only play stud or hold'em," he tells me, "so you should really practice those."

No problem. Practice is my middle name, and stud and hold'em are games I like. I spend thirty days on the couch, intent as ever.

The night before I leave I begin to wonder what kinds of clothes I should take with me. When my parents and aunts and uncles used to go on cruises, my mother would pack one gown for each night at sea. Those gowns had sequins or rhinestones, all shiny and bright. Tillie would come over with thick stacks of white tissue paper, and they would lovingly wrap each dress and place it gently in a suitcase. My mother would take two wigs, four pairs of high heels, and some bathing suits with matching cover-ups. Shorts and daytime dresses went on the top, with shoes wedged in the sides. I would sit on my parents' bed with all her jewelry spread out before me, and I would hold each piece up so my mother could choose the pieces that would go with each outfit. Those would be put in small satin drawstring bags. My mother always saved the best for last—her ruby ring and ruby earrings would go in a beautiful red velvet bag with her initials, SF, monogrammed in gold. It had a small gold bar that snapped it closed. I'd open and close it, open and close, that sound seeming to fill the room, until my mother would give me a look and I would settle down. I loved that bag, and would ask to pack it myself, making sure that each piece of jewelry was wrapped in tissue paper and placed inside just so. My mother would hand me a thick wad of money, and I would put the money in little piles, ones here, fives there, tens and twenties on my lap. I would make sure they were all facing the same way. When I got to the hundreds, usually three of them, I would flatten them out on the bed, smoothing them until they looked like they had been ironed. I would fold the money in half, and place that in the red velvet bag, too. That bag wasn't put into the suitcase; instead, it stayed safe in my mother's train-case, next to her Zippo and her cigarettes, her lipstick, and those endless packets of tissues.

But I don't envision gowns and wigs on this cruise, so I just grab a bunch of things out of my closet and stuff them in a suitcase.

Keith and Barbie are standing there when I get off the plane, holding a sign that says WELCOME MISS FRANKEL. They are practically jumping up and down. We are all so excited to be doing this together. Five whole days with nothing to do but relax and play poker.

Even though I've traveled extensively by myself, I worry about what it'll be like, playing with strangers. I've played with the guys on Wednesday nights, and other friends, and some of the kids, but I have never played with people I will probably never see again. Keith and Barbie know all the dealers and quite a few of the players, and I do not want to be sitting alone at dinner or trying to find my way around this enormous boat, so as we're walking up the gangplank, I turn to Keith and say, "Please don't leave me alone a lot. I don't know anybody else here."

"Okay," he says, "no problem." Barbie links her arm through mine and I start to feel a little better.

Keith and I go to our stateroom, but there must be some mistake. This is a closet. Where is our gigantic, spacious room? I take out the photos. It's the same room, but it's been shot at an angle that makes it look like it's about forty times bigger than it really is.

We're hysterical. The two of us and our suitcases can barely fit. We laugh for about an hour before Barbie comes and tells us that we have to go to the middle deck to learn what to do in case of fire. Keith and I roll our eyes, hurry her out of the room, and lock the door. We sit down on one of the tiny beds and get out a deck of cards. Keith starts to deal out some poker hands. It's not fifteen minutes later when we hear over the loud speaker, "Keith Berger, Martha Frankel, come to the deck. Keith Berger, Martha Frankel, come to the deck *immediately.*" By now we're crazed with laughter, but up we go. They have held up the other 450 passengers so that Keith and I can learn what to do in case of fire: we're to put on our fire vests and follow the other people up Stairway C. We are to stay close together and be orderly. Above all, we are not to panic. We will be told which lifeboats to get into. In the best of all worlds, this will take about forty-five minutes, during which a fire is raging around us. I will never do this. If there's a fire, I'm running to the closest deck, grabbing a life vest, and jumping overboard. Keith, too. We're good swimmers. My father taught us before we could walk. We can barely stay awake to listen to the captain's speech, and the minute he's finished, we race back to our room.

We play poker until it's time to meet Barbie, who has been in a training seminar all afternoon.

The first night I put on a pair of pants, a T-shirt, and a jacket. All of them are black, although not quite the same shade. Keith puts on a shirt that looks like it's been in a ball at the bottom of his suitcase. Actually, it *has* been in a ball at the bottom of his suitcase. We tell each other how good we look and head up to meet Barbie. As soon as she sees us, a frown overtakes her face.

"There's an iron in your room, I bet," she says.

I say, "Yeah, there's an iron. But who the hell's going to iron?"

Keith thinks that's really funny, but the glower Barbie gives us stops him cold.

"One of you can iron," she says through gritted teeth.

"Don't worry," Keith says, reaching for her hand. "We won't look like this again."

Dinner lasts for hours. There's shrimp and lobster, roast beef, steak, ham, desserts, piña coladas. The surprising thing is that the food is more than delicious. We meet the other dealers, and Barbie tells them to be especially nice because I'm a rookie. They tell me not to worry. "Tip them really well," Barbie whispers. I nod vigorously.

Barbie goes down to the casino first and comes back to report that there are six tables in the poker room, five- and ten-dollar minimums. They'll alternate between thirty minutes of hold'em and thirty minutes of stud. Keith says he's going to play in the higher-stakes game. I'm planning to play in the lower one. We finish dinner and head to the casino. I am assaulted by the noise as soon as I walk in. The room is enormous, with slot machines on all the walls, craps, blackjack, and roulette tables in the middle of the room, and hundreds of people milling around. Keith has to keep propelling me forward. He leads me toward a room in the back of the casino, separated from all the noise and mayhem. Compared to the main floor of the casino, the poker room feels like a chapel.

I ask one of the dealers to point me to the lower-stakes game. But as I go to sit down, Keith says, "No, come with me, play in the high-stakes game." I'm on pins and needles. Not only have I never played with strangers, I have never, ever played for this kind of money. Keith sits down next to me and says, "Don't worry, play conservatively, but be a little aggressive." I think about this. Can you be conservative and aggressive at the same moment? I don't think so, but I don't have the time to ask him to explain it to me.

We are by far the youngest people at the table, almost the youngest ones on the whole ship. There are lots of couples, lots of groups of friends. Everyone at our table introduces themselves and tells us a little about their life. Keith tells them that he's a gold-miner; no one flinches. I say that I do celebrity interviews, and immediately I am the most popular person on the boat. I tell them about how Anthony Hopkins called me at home a few hours after he won his Oscar, because I had predicted his win months before when I had met him for an interview in Santa Monica. I tell them about how weird and uptight Anne Rice was when I interviewed her, just because I asked if her husband, Stan, ever fucked her up the ass with a dildo, as many of the characters in her semipornographic stories do. I tell them about the amazing lunch that Oscar winner Juliette Binoche cooked for me in her home in France— avocado halves with aged balsamic vinegar, roast chicken with preserved lemons, and baby carrots fresh from the garden—and about how I almost came to blows with Roman Polanski when I met with him in Paris because he told me that women who don't have children are basically frigid bitches.

Everyone loves me!

Someone stop me, please. I rarely use my interviews as cocktail-party chatter, but I am so completely unglued that I just babble on and on. And my tablemates do seem very amused.

I'm having such a good time that I hardly play any poker. I win a few hands, lose a few hands, and basically just spend the night chatting, schmoozing. I move my seat next to the dealers', and ask them a million questions. I'm told that in this game you can ask to see a player's cards if they have stayed to the end, even though you are the winner and have turned your cards faceup. I learn that the dealers on this boat get to keep their own tips, while on some of the other cruises, they pool and split them with the other dealers. When I win I throw the dealer bigger tips than the other players, and they wish me luck.

The dealers rotate from table to table every half hour, and when Barbie finally gets to ours, it's hysteria. Within three minutes she knows everybody's name. She'll say, "Hey, Bob, the bet's to you." Or "Come on, Gorgeous George, bet your aces." Everybody loves her. When one guy throws her a five-dollar tip, he says, "Put it toward hair spray, babe." Her hair is already teased like a Jersey girl's.

All of a sudden I look at my watch and it's five in the morning. Five in the morning! This is the first time I've ever played poker all night. I don't even feel tired. I'm up about sixty bucks, Keith, six hundred. We go back to our room and sit up for hours while Keith tells me what I did right, what I did wrong, and what he expects me to learn while on this cruise. Then we fall into a deep, deep sleep, rocked by the waves.

When we get up the next day we're in Nassau. Barbie has left us a note that says not to wake her—she didn't get out of the casino till eight o'clock—so Keith and I go into town and buy bottles of perfume, a BAHAMIANS DO IT SLOWER baseball cap, a humungous straw hat, a few other hats that are simply hellacious, and a picture frame that says "Welcome to Nassau."

When we get back on the boat, neither of us really knows what to do with ourselves. We try lying at the pool, but the sun is relentless. Our air-conditioned room sounds good, but it's too cramped to relax in. The casino is closed, because they can only operate when we're out at sea, which won't happen till after dinner. We are wandering to and fro, hither and yon, feeling more and more like two of the Three Little Bears, when I run into one of the players I met last night, a funny, handsome guy named Jimmy who works as a purchasing agent at the Kennedy Space Center. Keith immediately dubbed him the Astronaut. The

Astronaut tells me that some of the other players are set-
ting up a game in an empty ballroom. It's illegal, and the
cruise ship doesn't condone gambling when in port, but
do I want to come play? I ask the stakes and he tells me
that they're quarter, half, dollar, which is the same stakes
I play with on Wednesday nights, and that it'll be dealer's
choice. I look toward Keith, but he tells me to go along
without him—he hates low-stakes games. He reminds me
to be back in the room by five. "So we can do the ironing,"
he says.

There are six other players, some I played with last
night. They deal a lot of games that I've never heard of,
but I do what I've been taught. Watch, fold, ask what usually wins in each game, wait until I feel like I understand
before I dive in. This sure beats exploring foreign locales.

The players at this table are a mixed bunch: the Astronaut; Lena and Jeff, a retired couple who play poker every
single day; and three men, completely drunk, who are college buddies from forty years before. The men admit that
they've been drinking since they got on the boat. Their
names are Larry, John, and Jake, but all their friends call
them the Harrys. Everyone's in a great mood and the
hours evaporate. I'm up about $125 when I realize it's time
to leave. "Why are you leaving when you're winning?"
one of the Harrys asks. I start to laugh. "Why, should I
wait till I'm losing?" I say. Everyone gets a confused look

on their faces. I will hear that same question—Why are you leaving when you're winning?—from dozens of people over the next few years.

When I get back to the room, Keith is waiting. He has set up the mini–ironing board on one of the beds, and holds a pile of clothes in one hand and a deck of cards in the other. "High card irons," he says.

He shuffles the cards and spreads them out on the bed. "Ladies first," he says with a smile.

I pick a four and start to laugh.

But he runs his hand over the cards as if he's Carnac the Magnificent, and when he finally pulls a card and turns over a two, I must say I'm not surprised.

I iron a shirt and a pair of slacks for him, a skirt and a blouse for me. It takes me over an hour.

When Barbie sees us she gives us a huge grin, and all that work suddenly seemed worth it. We have dinner with her and the Astronaut and some of the dealers as the boat moves out from shore, and are slowly joined by our new circle of friends. The Harrys keep urging everyone to have another drink—free booze and endless buffets seem to be a big part of the reason these people go on cruises. Nobody seems to notice that Keith and I never lift our glasses, Keith because he's never been a drinker, and me, because I stopped drinking when I started writing professionally: every night felt like a party, and every morning was a hangover nightmare. And it certainly doesn't hurt to be sober at a poker table full of drunks.

We chat until they announce that the casino is open, and then there's a mad dash to get a seat. The Astronaut and two of the Harrys are at our table, along with a few men we haven't seen before. The third Harry is at the blackjack table with a woman he met at dinner. We play for a few hours, and then Keith tells the dealer to mark our seats for a half-hour break.

I don't want a half-hour break. I'm doing well and having a great time, flirting with the Astronaut and making small talk. But I follow Keith outside and walk to the edge of the ship. He looks at me seriously and says, "I think the guy in the four seat and the guy in the eight seat are colluding." I had no idea that our seats have numbers, and Keith sees my confusion. "Count from the dealer and go clockwise," he says. "The guy to the dealer's left is in the one seat. There's something weird going on. Just watch them."

We go back into the poker room and retake our seats. I see which men Keith is talking about. They're both about fifty, and neither is particularly chatty. I try to see what they do when they're both in a hand, but I'm way too much of a novice to know about collusion, where two or more players signal each other so only the one with the strongest hand stays in against the other players, and I understand how it would work in the abstract, but I am not clear about how it would work here, now, with all these other players.

And as much as I like playing Inspector Clouseau, I never see them doing anything that would make me suspicious.

We play until the casino closes. We are both winners and go back to our room and pass out with piles of chips all around us.

I sleep till one o'clock in the afternoon, and when I go to meet Keith for lunch, I run into one of the Harrys, who tells me that a poker game is already under way. I grab a sandwich, kiss Keith, and go to the ballroom. I think I could stay on this boat for the rest of my life and be happy. Very happy. If Steve and my poker buddies were here, I'd never leave.

When I meet Keith back in the room later, he's wearing a little Rasta beanie that he bought in port that afternoon. He looks retarded.

"You really should have come with me today," he says, sulking.

"Poker or silly hats?" I say, holding my hands out in front of me as if I'm weighing something. "Poker or silly hats? Think I'll stick with poker."

After dinner Barbie hands me a bagful of casino chips, her tips, which she doesn't want to cash in till the last day. "Hide them," she says, "or Keith will spend them." Which is exactly true. I go back to the room and find a place where Keith will never think to look—I tape them to the bottom of the ironing board.

That night our poker table is full of our friends—the Astronaut and the Harrys, some of the other players we've met in the last few days. The Harrys keep talking about the wonderful comedians performing in the ship's theater, but no one makes a move to go see them.

We just play poker till the sun comes up.

I feel bad that I haven't been spending time alone with Keith, so I promise that we'll get off in port and go shopping together. But I don't. I go to the ballroom, where the Harrys tell me how much they missed me. I missed them, too. I like this game more than the evening games, when the stakes are much higher, the players more surly, and the friction thick as jam. Here there's a lot more kidding around, a lot more storytelling. Keith finds me there later. He holds up a large shopping bag. "Bought a fedora," he says proudly.

While I'm ironing our clothes that night, I ask Keith if he's ever colluded with anybody at poker, knowing that there was a year or so when he played every single day at Caesars Palace in Vegas. He says, "Never. Never. Poker is skill and luck. Your skill could be that you flirt and that puts people off their game. Your skill could be that you're funny and people are laughing and not paying attention. But anything that's not skill and luck is outside the realm." He tells me that he's had people approach him to collude, but even the man with a plan won't go there. "Then I'd have to give up playing, because I'd know I was a scumbag."

That night when Keith and I go to the poker room we see that the two guys we had been watching aren't even at the same table. We look at each other and roll our eyes. Wrong again.

When Keith and I take breaks, he tells me what I'm doing wrong.

"Why are you telling me all this?" I ask. "You're beating me."

And he says, "Are you kidding, baby? I want to beat you when you're really good."

This is something that will come up again and again in poker—people want to beat somebody who's good. They don't want to beat you because you're an idiot. It's the opposite of what I'd imagine, but I can see the logic. Keith wants me to be good so that when he takes my money he doesn't feel like he's robbing a blind woman.

Of all the advice he gives me, one thing stays in my head: "Never take your eyes off the table. You can talk, flirt, and do whatever you want, but never take your eyes off the chips and the other players' hands. First of all, they give away a lot with how they pick up their chips and how they handle their cards. Also, at your Wednesday-night game, you want to make sure that everyone is throwing in what they say they are. And, really, where else should you be looking? A deaf person can play poker as well as someone who's not, because talking is just bullshit at the poker table. Some people talk a lot to throw you off. Others just lie because they want to confuse you. But body language is ingrained, and it's easy to see once you understand its posture."

Everyone on the boat agrees that Barbie's the best dealer. They all know her by name, while the other eight dealers seem almost invisible. She makes four times the tips they do.

The next day is our last, and I play poker all day, and then again at night. I feel like I've been on this ship my whole life. I can barely remember what it looks like anywhere else. I can't remember what my own bed feels like. That tiny little room that Keith and I were "stuck in" now seems enormous.

Before we pack, I insist on reimbursing Keith for the plane ticket, pay for my half of the room, and leave enormous tips for all the waiters and chambermaids. Even after that, I still have a thousand dollars more than I came with. On the way out the door, I remember Barbie's box of chips and run back to grab them from under the ironing board. I go to the cashier, turn it into cash, and give her the money.

Keith and Barbie and I are almost the last ones off the boat, because Keith gets pulled aside and grilled by the customs agents. Barbie and I just stand quietly. As we start to walk down the gangplank, we see that a large crowd has gathered, waving. As we get closer it becomes clear that they are waving at me. As we kiss the Harrys and the Astronaut good-bye, and exchange phone numbers and take photos with our new best friends, I realize I am actually crying.

EIGHT

Lucky Lefty

The cruise brings my playing to a new level: I am much more self-assured, more apt to read someone the right way, and I win more. Plus I learn what to do when there's a problem, because I have read *The Rules of Poker* from cover to cover several times. The dealers on the cruise gave me the book as a present. *Once a waitress, always a waitress,* I like to say, and I never forgot that they live on their tips. Back home, knowing the rules gets me elected referee, settler of all arguments.

Have I mentioned the arguments? I don't think I've ever been in a poker game where there hasn't been one. My mother had told me stories about people who never spoke again because of blowouts they'd had at the poker table. "It was the forties, during the war," she told me one day when I was visiting. She lit one of her endless Kents and leaned in. "We were living on Long Island because Daddy was stationed out there. This man, Lou, and his wife, Esther, used to play with us every week. She was a very good player, and he was not. Every week she used to win and give him little digs. One night she said, 'Come on, Lou, speed it up. I could have a heart attack before you decide what you're doing.' And he said, 'I should be so lucky.' "

I laughed, and my mother said, "Well, Esther didn't think it was so funny. She threw her drink in his face. They never came back to the game, and a few months later we heard they got divorced. And then about ten years ago I heard this story about Jake—remember him, he used to live in our building in Miami?"

Of course I don't remember Jake. But I nod, because if I admit I don't, she'll go into a twenty-minute story about what he wore, where he ate, and what a bitch his sister-in-law was. Nobody in their right mind would question my mother's memory.

"Well," she says, "I heard that he and his brother had a fight at the clubhouse because the brother accused Jake of saying he had a flush when he didn't. Jake had already thrown his cards into the muck pile and no one at the table was exactly sure if he really had five spades, or just four

spades and a bunch of clubs. The brother grabbed him
and punched him. And these guys were well into their
seventies." My mother laughed. "Go figure," she said.

On the cruise I witnessed two heated arguments, one
at the next table between a couple and another player
who they accused of peeking at their cards. And one at my
table when a guy kept betting out of turn and one of the
Harrys lost it and started yelling at him. Both times I stood
up. Keith pulled me back into my seat. "Unless someone's
got a gun," he said out of the corner of his mouth, "stay
seated."

It's not all bonbons at the poker table, and I loved how
the dealers on the ship took control, laid down the law, and
created détente among the players.

I come back from the cruise feeling like an anthro-
pologist who has just returned from a foreign land with
intriguing tales of wild natives. I teach the guys every new
game I've learned, and they immediately become "our"
games. We give them nicknames like "rock 'n' roll" and
"the usual," because we start dealing them all the time.

I tell the guys about the Harrys, and admit that I only
got off the boat once and that I have no idea if the Bahamas were nice or not. And that I didn't care. No one at the
table thinks that's weird at all. We kid around about taking a cruise together, and I regale them with stories of lobster salads and all-day poker games. They want to know

more about the arguments, because we have our share of them, too.

In home games, most of the fighting is about dealer screwups, which can be monumental. I once was dealing a hand with the red deck, picked up the blue one in the middle of the hand, and dealt the last few cards from that deck. When I dealt the last card down, everyone realized that some cards were red and some blue. We all stared at the cards, amazed. Sal, who thought he had the best hand in the mixed-deck deal, didn't win the hand when I re-dealt it with only one deck. To circumvent his anger, I took fifteen dollars out of my pocket and gave it to him. Then I made the same mistake a few months later! When one of the players realized he had two aces of spades, we all laughed till we were crying. We began calling dealer mistakes "mooks," and they charitably christened me the Mook Adjuster. I am legendary in my small circle of friends.

There is always a way to sort out the disagreements, though, and I became the go-to girl for that.

Lefty is one of the people who starts a lot of the fights, always arguing that someone did something wrong, someone screwed up. I still haven't figured out how, but now I'm positive that he is cheating. Does he start the fights to take our attention away from this?

Finally Sal and I tell Michael our suspicions about

Lefty, and he starts watching him, too. One night he yells at Lefty to keep the cards down when he's dealing, as his hands keep getting higher and higher. Lefty just smiles. Now Michael and Sal are always telling him that he's shorting the pot, but he acts as if he doesn't hear them, either. When he's dealing, he talks too loud, moves his hands around erratically, and generally seems like he's trying to hypnotize us. It's so creepy that I wish I didn't have to watch. Confronting him seems out of the question, because the whole thing is so ugly.

Since the cruise, I never take my eyes off the table. I watch each player throw their chips in, making sure it's the right amount. I watch to see if anyone is cupping chips in their hands and only pretending to throw them in. Eventually they ask me to be the one who keeps track of the money and sells the players their chips. I laugh: this was my job at mah-jongg, too. But, then again, I was the one who kept track of the gin scores when Keith and I were kids. And I'm still the one who divides the checks in a restaurant.

During this time I start taking assignments again—I've learned all I can on the couch, and it's time for me to make some money. I travel to Los Angeles once a month or so, and start booking my trips from Thursday till Tuesday so I don't miss a Wednesday-night game. I do one of the first interviews with a nineteen-year-old Leonardo

DiCaprio, where we spend our time seeing who could spit furthest from my twelfth-floor hotel room. I win, hands down. I spend hours arguing politics with Cuban exile Andy Garcia, although I'm not quite sure why I'm arguing, because he makes perfect sense. I dance the conga with Christopher Walken, and go CD shopping with Jeff Bridges, who reintroduces me to Dusty Springfield and John Mayall. My stories take on a lighter, breezier tone, and my editors are really pleased. All of this is possible because I'm not really there. I seem present, but I'm thinking about poker all the time, and the rest of my life—work, family, friends—seems like filler. Pleasant filler, for sure, but spackle nonetheless.

At night, in strange hotel rooms, I read books on poker strategy. I learn about pot odds and money management. I dream of poker hands. While I'm doing the interviews, I imagine myself in high-stakes games. I have to stop myself from daydreaming long enough to ask interesting questions, which will get the celebrity I'm interviewing to give long, involved answers. Thank god for tape recorders.

This must be the way alcoholics feel—they look at you and nod, and the whole time they're thinking, *Shut the hell up and let me have a drink. Leave me alone so I can go back to the thing I love.*

My mother is one of the few people I like speaking with during this time. Early in the mornings I call her, and we

talk poker for hours. She can listen to me talk about different hands without ever getting bored, and makes me laugh
when she tells me her own poker nightmares.

◆ ◆ ◆

One night the phone rings while Sal and Karen are having
dinner with Steve and me. It's Robert, one of the guys who
joined our Wednesday-night game. Robert keeps saying
that he has something to tell me, but I can hear that he's
having a hard time getting to the point. He stammers
before finally blurting it out.

"Lefty's cheating," he says.

"I know," I answer.

I will be explaining those two words for years to come.

"You know? You know?" he repeats after a while, really
stammering now. "You know? You knew he was cheating
and you invited me into a game with him? What the hell's
wrong with you?"

I don't know what to say. I've known that Lefty was
cheating since the first night I played with him, and I can't
deny that. There are half a dozen guys who I invited to
play with us over time, and when they find out that I knew,
they are also furious with me. I'm still apologizing for it.

"I'm sorry," I tell Robert now.

"He's dealing off the bottom of the deck," Robert says.

This I did not know.

"No," I say. "That would be...that's so fucked up...no, I don't believe that."

"It's true," Robert says. "I watched him. I first heard it from Pete a while back. That's why Pete quit the game."

I try to remember—I thought Pete quit the game because of me.

"I watched Lefty last week," Robert says, "and I saw him do it a few times."

"Why didn't you say anything to him?"

Robert hangs up on me.

I go in to the dining room and tell Sal. We both groan. We call Michael and make plans to meet him the next day at his restaurant. Sal and I spend the whole night talking about it, long after Karen has gone home and Steve has gone to bed. It was one thing when we thought he was shorting the pot a quarter now and then, but dealing off the bottom of the deck—that's a whole new level of cheating. This is a skill you have to perfect. This sickens me, his premeditation and outright plan to cheat his friends. He had to spend hours on the couch—I can imagine that part perfectly—going over it again and again. Sal and I try it: we can't even figure out how to hold the cards.

The next day we have lunch with Michael. None of us knows what to do. It's really the worst for Sal, because he and Lefty go way back. But Sal is furious and wants to catch him as much as Michael and I do. We talk about different ways to approach it—should we just go to him and tell him that we know? But we all know that won't work. We realize that the only way to stop him is to literally catch him with the cards in his hands.

We spend hours talking, but can't think of a good way for this to work. We decide to meet again the next day. When we go back I bring a deck of cards and we keep passing it around, trying to figure out how he does it. If he's really dealing from the bottom of the deck, the easiest thing would be to know what the bottom card is when he's dealing, and then see if it winds up in someone's hand. But how?

What we finally decide is that the person who is cutting for Lefty's deal will flash the other players the card that will be on the bottom of the deck, so that everyone but Lefty will know what that card is before he starts dealing. And if that card should show up in a hand, we'll know where it came from. The plan also involves taking Lefty's attention away from the deck at the same time everyone else is watching it. I don't think this will work—paying attention is not really anyone's strong suit. Except mine.

In my heart, I think all of our talking and planning is bullshit. First, I cannot wrap my mind around the idea of Lefty dealing from the bottom of the deck. It just seems so Old West. Does this really happen at a friendly, low-stakes, neighborhood game? And if it is true, I doubt we will ever be able to catch him. Obviously he's a lot trickier than us.

The next game is a couple of days away, and all Sal and I do is obsess about catching Lefty. Of course it snows that Wednesday and we have to cancel. Steve and I are going on vacation the next Wednesday, and I ask Sal and Michael if they want to wait until I get back. But they want to put our plan into action as soon as they can. Lotsa luck, I think.

At the next game, the only guy who shows up besides Lefty, Sal, and Michael is Doc. Sal takes Doc aside and tells him what's going on.

I call Sal the minute I land in Puerto Rico. "Holy shit, I wish you'd been there," he tells me. "We played all night and nothing out of the ordinary happened. Everyone kept flashing the bottom card at each other, but it never wound up in the game. And then about midnight, when we were all ready to go home, Lefty was dealing and I saw that the bottom card was a nine of clubs. Lefty's first two up cards were the nine of diamonds and the nine of hearts. And at the end of the hand he turns over all of his cards and says, 'Bad news for you guys. Lucky Lefty's got four nines.'"

I moan.

"I know," Sal says. "I threw my cards down in disgust. 'You know, Lefty,' I told him, 'I really, until this minute, didn't believe it.' And he said, 'Didn't believe what?' 'That you cheated,' I said. He got really huffy, told us to go fuck ourselves, grabbed his coat, and left. Michael and Doc and I were just freaking out, not sure if we should feel good that we caught him, or awful that he was cheating. We were standing around talking when the door flew open. Lefty came storming back in, and we all sort of backed away. He walked over to us, took all the money out of his pocket, and laid it on the table. 'Listen, I'm sorry,' he said. All I could think to say was, 'Are you admitting it?' Lefty said, 'Yeah, I'm really sorry.' And then he left again."

"I'm shocked," I say. "I never thought we'd catch him."

"Me either," Sal says. "I'm relieved, but the whole thing sucked."

A few days later Sal calls me back and says that Lefty had just called him. "He said he was sorry again, and that he went to see a therapist."

"That couldn't hurt," I say.

When I get back from Puerto Rico, Lefty calls to apologize to me. He tells me that he's making headway with the shrink. I try not to giggle. I have a million questions to ask, but I don't. That will take years.

◆ ◆ ◆

Over the next decade, I run into Lefty a few times a year. He's always overly friendly, leaning in to kiss me and talking loudly to whoever happens to be standing around. I never know what to do during these encounters. I feel like I'm carrying a huge secret for him, a secret I wish I didn't know. We live in a small town, and I'd like to let bygones be bygones.

◆ ◆ ◆

Almost ten years to the day after they caught him cheating, I call Lefty and ask if I can take him out for breakfast. I tell him I'd like to talk to him, face-to-face. We make a date to meet the next morning.

He's already sitting at a table with coffee and a Danish when I get to the Bread Alone café. He's cool as a cucumber, hardly even glancing up when I sit down. "What's up?" he asks casually.

"There's some things I want to ask you. It's about poker . . ."

"I figured," he says, although he doesn't seem at all uncomfortable.

"I was wondering if my coming into the game made you start cheating . . ."

"No," he says. "Why?"

"I thought maybe losing to a girl was worse than losing to one of the guys."

"No, I just didn't like losing at all."

"Did you switch to different games because they would be easier to cheat at?"

"No," he says.

"Michael says that when you played with us, he always did really well. He wonders if you were helping him out in some way that he didn't know about . . ."

"No, no. I loved all of you the same."

I feel a smile start to form. I have never heard the word *love* used quite this way. "Did you have to teach yourself to deal from the bottom of the deck?"

"Nope, I've always done magic. I've always been good with cards."

I think back to what I told Karen after the first night I played with him. The rabbit out of his shirt. Misdirection. Magic. How could I have been so stupid?

There's silence for a while.

"In the game I play in now . . ." he begins.

"Wait, you play poker again?"

"Oh, sure. It's a really low-stakes game. I play with the guys I work with in the city, and a big part of it is that we make these gourmet meals. It's a very cool game. I would never do what I did before."

I imagine Lefty playing poker with new guys, people who don't know what to watch for, people who trust him. I don't know what to say. "Did you cheat when the Ref was in the game?" I finally ask. The Ref started the poker game

I play in. He was a local hero who died a few years before I started playing. He was forty-two years old. Sal and Michael always told me stories about what a great player he was, and how he used to say *Play till you lose.* By that he meant that if you have the best hand, play until someone has a better one...and then fold. But people misunderstood him to mean *Play until you win,* which kept them in hands long after they should have left. One of the nicest compliments Michael ever paid me was when he said that my poker playing reminded him of the Ref's. I don't believe that Lefty had the balls to cheat when the Ref was around.

"I always thought the Ref was cheating," Lefty says.

"What?" I sputter.

"Yeah, I thought he might be, because he always won," he tells me, coolly.

The Ref has been dead for years—does this scumbag have no respect? Does he think that the whole world cheats, that the only reason he had to stop playing with us is because he got caught? My leg starts tapping like some drummer on speed.

"I win a lot," I say, my jaw clenching. "And I never cheat."

He looks at a point somewhere to the right of my head. "Whatever you say."

"I knew you were cheating the first night I played with you," I say hostilely.

"No I wasn't," he says quickly.

"Yes, you were. You were shorting the pot."

He shrugs. "Everyone does that."

"No, they don't." Now I *am* shouting.

Lefty picks up his newspaper and starts to read. I get up and pay for our breakfast. I can't get away from him quick enough. It's like he's full of a spice I hate, and when I walk away the scent lingers.

He will never understand that his cheating disrupted our whole game, that for weeks, months, and even years, it was all we could talk about. His cheating made us suspicious of every new player who came into the game. He was one of the guys, one of our friends, someone we shared a laugh and a meal with, and the whole while he was thinking about how to bilk us out of a few extra dollars.

Loyalty and friendship are obviously not his strong suit.

NINE

Coming Home

The summer after the hoo-ha with Lefty, Susan Brown, a writing teacher I adore, invites me to a workshop she's giving. It will be at the home of memoirist Linda Atkins, for ten days, in the middle of the summer, in a three-story house in Ventnor, New Jersey, a few paces from the ocean. I'll have my own room, with windows facing the shore. There will be six of us, including one writer who will also be our cook. It will cost me $1,200, which includes all our meals. What's to think about?

From the minute I arrive I feel like the most pampered, wanted guest in the world. The whole day is mine to sit on the beach and write. Every morning I take a little sand chair, an umbrella, a legal pad, a huge bottle of water, and find a spot where I can stay for hours. I am surrounded by grandmothers and their grandkids, whose parents must all be in New York City working. The kids make sand castles while their grandmas knit. At least twice a day the women will say, "Sweetie, do you want some ice cream?" This is exactly what the bungalow colony was like when I was kid: during the week all the fathers were gone and it was only mothers and grandmothers and children. My mother would play mah-jongg by the pool all day, and at night we would sit outside and eat ice cream. On Friday mornings my grandmother would help my mother roll her hair into tight little cylinders, which they secured with bobby pins. My mother kept them in until an hour before my father drove into the parking lot, when she would pull out the pins and run her hands through her hair until she looked like a movie star. It was a wonderful, carefree time, and being in Ventnor feels like coming home.

After glorious, delicious dinners—crab cakes with sautéed baby artichokes, fresh potato pierogies with gobs of sour cream, chicken roasted with garlic and lemon—we read aloud from our works-in-progress, and everyone but me gets completely soused, drinking from the cases of wine they've brought along. One of the other writers is ballerina Allegra Kent, who is writing about her days as George Balanchine's muse, a book that would eventually become *Once a Dancer....* After some initial awkwardness between us, mostly caused by my not knowing where to look when Kent would wrap her leg around her neck and turn herself into a human pretzel during dinner, we become inseparable and spend many hours walking the beach, talking about our lives. Kent has been a dancer since she was a child; she is at once limber and fragile, and there is something otherworldly and wonderful about her. Brown is a funny earth mother who is constantly making sure that everyone is okay, and as much as everyone might drink at night, she is the first one up in the morning, full of wry observations as well as concise changes she thinks we need to make in our stories. I am working on a rough outline of my screenplay, although mostly I stare into space and think about poker. Atkins, a psychoanalyst by trade, has a rapier wit that has us all in stitches most evenings, and is possibly the most understanding person who has ever lived. It's girls' camp, with writing thrown in for good measure.

Ventnor is three miles south of Atlantic City. We can see the red neon signs—TRUMP! CAESARS! HILTON!— from the boardwalk in Ventnor. Atkins likes to take long runs early in the morning, and I am the one who drives up to Atlantic City to pick her up so she can be back in time for breakfast. Her husband, Jerry, is a psychiatrist, sculptor, and real estate mogul who comes down to Ventnor on Friday nights and spends all day Saturday and a few hours Sunday playing poker. Their joke is that he's the only one at the casino who stands up at five p.m., no matter how he's doing, and goes to meet his wife for dinner. Atkins asks if I ever played at the casinos, and I shake my head, no.

But after a few days, when everyone has heard endlessly about my obsession with poker, they all agree that we should skip dinner at home and venture north. We eat at a lousy Chinese restaurant and then walk around the craps tables and slot machines at the Taj Mahal. I don't spend a penny at any of these games. They are for suckers. If the casino can win, it will win. Poker is the only game where the player has a chance, because you are playing against each other, not the house. Our writers' group is in a stupor: the music is pounding, the machines are lighting up and making strange sounds, the carpet is busy, an orange-and-purple paisley. Eventually we stumble upon the poker room. "Go ahead," my cheering section says. "Sit down and play."

Although I have been on the cruise and played with strangers, I had Keith there to explain the lay of the land. Here I feel completely out of my league, as if after a few flying lessons on a small, lightweight plane, I am now being given a 747 to fly cross-country. Please fasten your seat belts.

I'm not sure where to sit. I'm not sure where you buy chips. I look around the room and there are fifty or sixty tables full of players, mostly men, an older woman or a young girl here and there. I finally see a woman who has a look of authority, so I go over and stand near her until she notices me.

"What can I do for ya?" she asks.

"Can I get a seat?"

She points to the front of the room, where a crowd of men have congregated. Every one of them is smoking a cigarette. I wander over cautiously and notice a big white board with initials on it. A woman with a Sharpie in her hand looks my way. "Whadda ya want?" she asks in full-on Brooklynese.

I hesitate. My whole writing group is huddled behind me, waiting for me to gain entrance into this kingdom, only it seems I don't know the password.

"Honey, we got stud and we got hold'em," the woman says quickly. "Dollar to five, five and ten, ten and twenty, and above. Pick your poison."

"Stud," I stammer. "One to five." I assume this means that the bets range from one to five dollars, but I'm not absolutely sure. The woman points, and I follow her finger, where a tall man in a tuxedo is waving to me. I go to him, with the writers following, and he points to a seat at one of the tables. We all let out the same sound, a cross between a cheer and a yelp, like a puppy who gets his foot caught in the door but still wants to run outside so he can chase a cat. I sit down and smile at my fellow players, who barely glance my way. I take a hundred-dollar bill out of my pocket and lay it in front of me. The dealer takes it, hands me some chips, and, BANG, just like that, I'm playing poker with the big boys.

The writers pull up some chairs around me and lean in whenever I get my cards. I show them what I have and they all try to keep a straight face. I play very few hands in the first hour, just watching and waiting until I get something great. And until my breathing gets even. And the sweat that forms on my hands evaporates. I cannot ever remember being this scared.

After a while the writers get bored and head back into the casino. When the chair next to the dealer opens, I move there, so I can ask my many questions and have a little help if I need it.

The dealer, it turns out, is a complete jerk, loud and obnoxious, dealing so fast that cards are careening around the table. More than one player will ask him to slow down, but he's too busy flirting with another dealer at the next table to care what we think. I notice that the players throw him half a dollar when they win, and I wonder if this is the going rate. Luckily for all of us, the dealers change every half hour and the next one is a doll. I tell him that this is my first time at a casino, and he laughs. "Probably not the last," he ventures. He is squat and soft, and his name tag says Von.

I let Von peek at my cards while he's dealing. I win three

big pots in a row, and tip him four dollars after each hand. I feel like we have some kind of mojo going, like I can just keep winning if he keeps dealing. But unfortunately, he, too, leaves after thirty minutes. As soon as the new dealer, Pauline, sits down, the other players start yelling at me. "You tipped him too much," they say. "Don't be an idiot." They are enraged, as if I had been using their money to pay my bills. I don't say a word, partially because I think they're schmucks, but mostly because I'm mortified. Have I stepped over some imaginary line, thereby showing myself to be a novice? And this when I finally felt like a player.

I play for another hour, and things do not improve with my tablemates. I try to make small talk, but they ignore me. I have tipped too much, and am marked. And then the writers come back. As soon as I see them, I yell, "Time to go," with such a hale and hearty voice that they agree. I pick my chips up in two hands, not noticing the clear plastic racks that are piled by all the tables, and motion for the writers to pick up the rest. We head toward the cashier. Chips are spilling everywhere, and the writers are picking them up as if they're my handmaidens. When we drop the last of them on the counter in front of the cashier, I am panting. "How'd you do?" my friends ask.

"I know I'm ahead but I'm not sure how much." I am just so glad to be away from that angry pack of men, from their derision and the shame I felt for not knowing casino protocol. When the cashier hands me back $380 I almost scream. The writers do. We all start jumping up and down, and head back to Ventnor, everyone talking about what we would do if we won the lottery.

The next morning, everyone cannot stop talking about my huge win. "Let's go back tonight," Susan says, and they all agree. It's raining and no one feels like writing, so we sit around all day and I teach them to play poker. Some of the women have played before, and some have never played cards in any form. How much fun is this? I call Steve and tell him what fun we're having playing poker. "Wait," he says, "I thought you were there to write." He sounds surprised, but I don't have the time to explain. We head back to the Taj after dinner, and this time I swagger right in, just like the rest of the guys. I go put my initials on the board and wait for a seat to open. A couple of the writers do, too, and we pat each other on the back.

Within two hours, the writers want to leave. Since we're all in one car, I leave, too. But after we get home and everyone is in their pajamas, I realize that I'm not remotely tired. I wait till I hear the last of them go to their rooms, and I slip out of the house. I could tell them that I'm going back to Atlantic City, but I don't. I sneak out the door and drive back to the Taj.

I get a seat right away, and wind up at a table with another snarly group of men. Every hand ends in a screaming match. In the casinos, the fights start for a variety of reasons: the dealer does something wrong and a supervisor has to be called over, by which time every player at the table is shouting to be heard and mayhem breaks out. The pit bosses will stop the game, make everyone shut up, and ask the dealer what happened so they can sort it out. Sometimes, when no one can give them a clear explanation, they will go to the cameras that are above each table and rerun the video to see what transpired. But this is rare and can stop the game for an hour or so, during which time the players must stay in their seats and wait. Sometimes one player thinks another doesn't turn their cards over fast enough. "Stop slow-rolling me!" they'll scream. Or the players are losing and edgy, and yelling seems like a good way to let off steam. There are players who fling their cards across the table or at the dealer or another player when they lose. Some slam their chips down as hard as they can, and others who bait each other. Sometimes the dealer will ask them to stop, but it rarely deters them.

I am not one of those players. I never yell, I never fling cards, I never call anyone bad names. I may think it, sure, but I know that it screws me up more than it screws the other player. *Never gloat, never complain.*

But this table is out of control. They fight with the dealer, they fight with each other, and they are ready to chew me up and spit me out. I try flirting, I try chatting, I try making small talk with the dealer. But no one will bite. The odd thing is that I start to do well, even though I am so uncomfortable. The more I win, the more they hate me. I get cards flung in my face, get yelled at by a guy whose mouth is foaming, get called a bitch and a moron.

You're welcome.

I arrive home just as everyone is finishing breakfast. They are surprised to see me walking through the front door, but when I take six hundred-dollar bills out of my pocket and start waving them over my head, everyone starts clapping.

I sleep all day, take the writers out to dinner, and head back to the poker room. Which is what I do every day and night until it's time to go home. I don't get much writing done, but I bond with the writers, and head home three thousand dollars richer.

A few weeks later I go to Los Angeles to interview Jennifer Beals, whom I had met through mutual friends a few years before. As I'm checking into the Mondrian Hotel, I hear a bunch of handsome men talking about going to play poker. I linger and loiter until I hear them mention Hollywood Park. Finally I go over and ask them where, and what, is Hollywood Park?

They are more than happy to explain that it's a racetrack with a card room a few miles from LAX. Would I like to come along?

I have been traveling for over twelve hours, I am tired and cranky, I probably smell. Sure, why not?

I love these guys. They're in town for an amateur boxing event. They talk poker nonstop, and tell me that cards are legal all throughout the state of California, and that there are a lot of card rooms right outside of L.A. No slots or craps, but cards in many forms, especially poker.

Who knew? I stay there with the boxers till three in the morning, go back to the hotel for a few hours of sleep, and then pick up Jenny Beals. I convince her that we should do the interview at Hollywood Park. When we walk in, dozens of Japanese men start yelling, *"Flashdance! Flashdance!"* Jenny signs some autographs while I get a seat at a stud table. Jenny pulls up a chair behind mine, and we spend a few hours talking and laughing while I play.

This is the most fun I've ever had doing an interview.

TEN

Poker Slut

I take as many assignments in Los Angeles as I can. I do my interviews over lunch, and promptly head back to my hotel room, napping till nine o'clock. By eleven p.m. I'm heading to Hollywood Park, or to Larry Flynt's new Hustler Casino, or to the Commerce. I purposely arrive when I know some of the other players are getting tired, when they're bleary-eyed from sitting at the tables for hours, while I'm Miss Wide-Eyed and Perky. I leave by five in the morning, no matter how I'm doing, so I can get back to my room and get some sleep before I have to go to work.

I meet players at each casino who recognize me from trip to trip, and I start to think of them as friends. Good friends. One night at Hollywood Park I am playing stud with a table made up mostly of Korean men and women. They are speaking English and are very pleasant to one another and to anyone else who sits down, but not one of them will talk to me. Or even look in my direction. This despite the fact that I keep asking questions, trying to draw them out. Being ignored is a new one for me. I have been avoided, maybe—ignored, never. I'm baffled. I keep at it, until one of the women points her long red finger-nail in my face and says, "It's because you wear all black. It's bad luck. No one wants to acknowledge bad luck." I'm shocked—black is, after all, the official uniform of most New Yorkers. But I'm a girl who listens and can learn from her mistakes. I buy a bunch of sweaters, low cut and bejeweled, in a variety of colors. I become the right-hand woman to all the Koreans.

Although I lose sometimes, I am a winner far more often, and for the first time in my life I have more money than I ever imagined. My work is going great, my bills are paid, and I always have a wad of cash in the small red velvet purse my mother gave me when I first started playing poker. She took it out of the closet on one of my visits, unwrapped it from layers of white tissue paper, and handed it to me like a samurai giving his son his first sword. "I know how much you always loved this," she said when I gasped, both of us remembering how I would pack her jewelry in it with such pride. She rubbed it lovingly, the SF a little worn now. "I thought I'd leave it for you when I died, but this is better. I think it has some good luck in it."

Sometimes Steve comes with me to L.A., where he immerses himself in car culture. I go to the casinos during the day when he's in town, while he goes to hot-rod shows and the Petersen Automotive Museum, which showcases some of his car art. He came with me to Hollywood Park once and seemed appalled by all the televisions showing horse racing, the people screaming at each other, the thick smoke in the air. But I convince myself that he secretly felt proud that I am at home in places he would never step into.

I keep wishing that I didn't have to go so far away to play, and that I could play more often. Even Atlantic City and Foxwoods Casino are a good four hours away from my home.

I tell myself I need to play more often because I'm researching that screenplay. I barely remember what the story was supposed to be about, but, damn it, I am a serious researcher. I have to tell Randy something soon, too, because he figures I must have notebooks full of ideas, when all I really have is a great knowledge of poker hands.

It's during this period that an unbelievable thing happens: the whole world starts playing poker! This isn't just my imagination. Dozens of new card rooms open in California. They are legal and upscale. And another breed of poker player is born. This player is apt to be a young man, wearing his baseball cap turned backward. These players only know how to play one game—Texas hold'em. In this game, you get two hole (down) cards, and then a series of five cards is turned faceup in the middle of the table: first, three cards (the flop), then another (the turn), and then the final card (the river). These up cards are the community cards, and you try to make the best hand between your hole cards and the community cards.

These new players start overrunning the card rooms in California and the casinos in Atlantic City. They are very aggressive, and more concerned with how cool they look while shuffling their chips than how well they play their cards. The old-time players hate their swagger, because they say a monkey could be trained to play hold'em well. These older players would rather play stud, a slower game that requires a higher degree of skill. But the hold'em players start to show up in droves, and it's often hard to find another game.

I like hold'em well enough, and these young guys don't scare me one bit. They don't kibitz a lot and are rude and mean to each other, and very critical of other players. It's as if they think that makes them better players. But I'm happy to play with them even though they dismiss women in general, and me in particular, because they think all blondes are ditzy. All the better when I walk out of there with their money.

Steve and I take a spontaneous trip up the California coast with Chris and Annie Flanders. We are celebrating Chris's successful heart transplant and his recovery from a debilitating stroke. Steve drives, and Chris sits in the front seat and works the radio. In the back, Annie leafs through endless newspapers and guidebooks to find us motels and good restaurants, and I watch for animals. I spot hawks and owls, sea lions and horses. One day I shout, "Look, a zebra!" and we watch it lazily walk across a great expanse of lawn. At night, in our motel rooms, we play gin rummy and laugh. The manager at the motel in Monterey mentions that there's a card room up the road. I'm thrilled. "It's on both sides of the street," he tells me. "You can't miss it." But I do—not one, not two, but three times. I go back to the hotel and he reiterates the same directions. I'm determined to find it, and finally do. It turns out to be a little bit bigger than my coat closet. There's one card table, and a bunch of quiet Native Americans hunched over their cards. They play hold'em as if it were a religion. I play till four in the morning, leave with a hundred and forty more than I came with, and the next day bring Annie and Chris and Steve back to see this amazing place. The same guys are still playing. One of them asks, "Hey, Martha, you gonna sit and play awhile?" But I tell them that we have to get on the road. Neither the Flanders family nor Steve say a word till we are safe in the car. "You came here, you saw that place, and you actually stayed?" Chris says as he and Steve share a look. But I felt comfortable there, happy and at ease.

Another time I tag along with Chris and Annie to Santa Barbara. Annie keeps talking about the delicious dinners we'll have and the hours of relaxing and daydreaming on the beach. Which I never see, because I find an Indian casino a few miles away. I play poker all night and sleep all day.

Back in L.A., I go to the Hustler Casino in the middle of a deluge. The rain makes everyone in Los Angeles crazy; oil starts seeping up out of the pavement and the roads become a slick mess. But the poker room has a weather system all its own, and tonight the forecast is clear and calm.

Till I notice the gun. Either that, or this guy has the funniest-looking wad of cash I've ever seen. He's about six-five, with a neck as big as both my thighs together. His Oakland Raiders T-shirt is bursting at the seams. His skin is so black it's purple, and he sneers through lidded, droopy eyes. If he's a gangbanger, he's not subtle: he's draped in gold chains, and has a beeper and a cell phone, both of which he's constantly working. Every half hour he leaves the table, signals for some underling, and comes back, stuffing cash in his pocket. He winks at me, showing his gold caps.

I'm wearing cleavage, attitude, and what might be, anywhere but here, a bit too much perfume. The rest of the guys at the table are white and nervous. Just the way I like them. It occurs to me that I should leave, go home now and count my winnings. But the stack of chips in front of me represents more money than I made my first year as a professional writer, and I'm loath to leave this mother lode. For about an hour I play very few hands and just watch him. He's good, which surprises me. He looks lazy but his mind is sharp. He doesn't talk much, doesn't ask a lot of idiotic questions. Best of all, he doesn't answer the other players' foolish questions, which seems to give them encouragement. I imagine they think he can't follow their superior logic. When he wins, they call it luck; when he loses, they point out that he shouldn't have been in the hand.

When he winks at me the next time, I hold his gaze and give him a huge smile. I want him on my side.

It works. Within an hour, he and I have broken two guys, who leave the table dejected. When the loser to my right throws in the last of his chips, the giant stands up, stretches those enormous arms, and slowly tosses a coin in front of the empty seat, signaling his intention to move closer to me.

I'm praying I have him figured right, that he's not going to be the one who follows me out in the parking lot and knocks me on the head to get my money. Or worse.

The poker room is still buzzing about a man named John who started flirting with a woman at his table and decided to take her to a motel. On the way, she asked to stop at a convenience store for a pack of cigarettes. When John got out of the car to get them, the woman's boyfriend came up behind him, shot him in the head, stole his money, and took off with the girlfriend in John's car.

So I'm cautious, not paranoid, but careful to cover my bases. When I left my hotel room I slipped the key in my bra, wrote the room number on my bikini line in case I forgot it, put two hundred-dollar bills in my left pocket and three twenties in my right. The rental car stayed in the hotel garage, and I took a cab to the casino, as I intend to do on the way back. I figure if I stay near the security guard on this end and the hotel doorman on the other, I've got the odds in my favor. But now, with this colossus sniffing my neck, I think I might not be cautious enough.

"Melvin," he says, sticking out his hand.

I almost laugh—it's the name of one of my Jewish uncles. But his presence discourages laughter. I wonder if

I should tell him my name, or is that just trouble? But he doesn't seem to expect it.

"Well, New York," he drawls, looking me up and down, "you a professional?"

Now I don't hesitate to tell him the truth. "No way. I just learned a couple of years ago." He looks at me hard, trying to figure out if I'm playing him. I don't tell him about how long it took me to remember that three-of-a-kind beats two pairs.

Finally Melvin smiles. "Does your momma know you're here so late?" I ignore him. I make small talk, flirt a little, don't get offended when he asks me if I've ever had a black man. I don't want to sleep with Melvin, and the truth is that if it was just me and him, I'd try to get as much of his money as I could. But with all these fish circling us, Melvin and I can build our stacks on them.

For three hours we sit side by side, getting friendlier with each deal. I double my money; Melvin triples his. In no way do we collude—it just makes it easier if you have someone at the table that you like, because the other players start gunning for both of you and that throws them off. At three in the morning I'm getting tired, so I stand up and bid Melvin good night.

"Your momma expecting you?" he asks with a leer. I can't help but laugh; Melvin's obviously never met *my* mother.

I go to Vegas to write about the American Booksellers convention, and after schlepping books around all day, at night I play poker. One night I decide to play in the highest-stakes game I've ever played in, a $10/$20 hold'em game. Everyone at the table is plastered. I mean slurring, falling-off-their-chairs drunk. But they're very funny and I hold my own for an hour or so. I am sitting next to the dealer and having a great evening when one of the players, a man about fifty or so, sticks his tongue out at me and starts rolling it around, as if we're having wild sex. I look around to see who else is watching, but no one else sees him. He does it again. And then again. I ignore him, blushing and trying not to look his way, but he keeps it up.

Finally I point to him while his tongue is hanging midair. "What's that about?" I ask loudly. Everyone at the table turns to see him. They begin chuckling. He turns scarlet. "Do you think that's funny?" I ask, baiting him.

He doesn't say a word.

"Or sexy? Because if you think that's sexy, you're delusional." He starts twitching, and I expect him to leave the table, but he doesn't. He just glares at me.

When a new dealer comes to our table, I whisper about the tongue guy, and the dealer starts laughing, too. Tongue Guy is so mad at me that he starts to play lousy hands, just completely on tilt.

Four or five hands later, I get a pair of tens as my hole cards. I flash them to the dealer, who rubs my leg with his under the table. It's not sexual, or at least that's the way I choose to read it. I want to bet my tens, but the four players before me, including Tongue Guy, raise and re-raise, so all I can do is call. The flop—the three cards that are turned over all at once after the first round of betting—is ten, ten, ace. I have four-of-a-kind, the best hand I have ever had at a casino. I will my legs to be still.

Tongue Guy bets, and I imagine that he has a pair of aces, which would give him an aces-over-tens full house. The only thing that could beat me is if another ace comes up, and he'd have four aces. Everyone before me raises and re-raises, so again I just call. I figure that the other three guys might have picture cards and are hoping to catch a straight or a full house. Nobody knows that I have four-of-a-kind, and I doubt they think Tongue Guy has a huge full house already. Whatever they have, not one of them folds. The next card is a king. Every bet costs each of us eighty dollars, and yet all five players stay. The last card is a jack. If someone had a queen and an ace, or a queen and a nine, they would have a straight. Which doesn't touch my four-of-a-kind, but none of the other players knows what I have. No one folds.

There's over thirteen hundred dollars in the pot when Tongue Guy turns over his pair of aces and throws them into the center of the table, triumphant. He is sneering at me, but when he looks down and sees my pair of tens, he freezes. He looks quickly back at the community cards and then at me. The other guys start hooting and hollering, showing their picture cards, talking about the straights or full houses they had. As the dealer is about to push my fortune toward me, Tongue Guy picks up a handful of chips and throws them at me. Some land on the table, some on the floor, and some on top of the tray of chips that the dealer has in front of him. Tongue Guy starts screaming, "You stupid cunt! Why didn't you bet?" I could point out that I never had the chance, but all I do is smile. And then he reaches over and tries to get his errant chips from the dealer's tray.

This turns out to be a very, very bad idea. Within seconds two security guards have pinned him to the table. I scream, and so do some of the other players, but the dealer tells us to just relax and stay in our seats.

They take Tongue Guy away. In my wildest dreams this confrontation couldn't have ended better. One of the supervisors comes over to gather the chips that were in front of Tongue Guy. Every single person in the poker room is looking at our table. The casino bosses come over and tell us that we have to wait while they look at the tape to determine how much money was in the pot, but we are too busy going over and over what everyone had, and why they were still in the hand, to care how long this takes. One of the guys says, "Holy shit. That was the wildest hand I've ever played."

An hour later they come back to tell us that there was fifteen hundred on the table when they took Tongue Guy out. All of that is mine. Tongue Guy had unintentionally given me an extra two hundred. Now I love him. The chips that fell on the floor and into the dealer's tray stay with the casino. Everyone at the table starts clapping. I give the dealer three hundred dollars, and he leans over to kiss me. I throw each of the players a twenty-five-dollar chip, Tongue Guy's money for us all to enjoy. They order another round of drinks. I play for a few hours more, and when I start to gather my belongings, one of the players says, "Why are you leaving when you're winning?" I don't answer.

I fly to London to interview Bruce Willis, and meet a guy in first class who starts talking to me about poker. By the time we've landed at Heathrow, he's invited me to his house to play the next night. His friends are all uptight, buttoned-down businessmen, but I have a great time and no one seems to mind that I win over a hundred pounds.

When I'm home for a few weeks I go to Atlantic City. My mother is on oxygen most of the time and is beginning to lose her sight, but she's so happy every time I pick her up in Baltimore and we head up the highway to Jersey. This is a woman who normally goes to sleep at eight o'clock; in Atlantic City, I have to pry her away from the slot machines at three in the morning. She has switched from blackjack and craps to the slots because of her vision, but over breakfast one morning I teach her to play hold'em. I explain that, in a way, it's like crack cocaine—very fast, very mindless, and impossible to stop. The perfect game for a generation that grew up with MTV, fast computers, and instant messaging. My mother, who has never taken drugs and had one whiskey sour sometime in the mid-1960s, who has never been on the computer and doesn't know what a music video is, totally understands.

That night we venture to the poker room together. The other players are urging her to hurry up, hurry up, hurry up. But my mother is intimidated by exactly no one. She takes her time, plays her cards right, and wins two hundred dollars. I proudly push her wheelchair back to our room.

I take her to Atlantic City a lot that year. She makes friends with some of the dealers and more than a few of the casino supervisors. They make sure that her wheelchair fits comfortably at the tables, and that she has her trusted cup of coffee by her side at all times. They wheel her into the hallway when she wants a cigarette—a small thing like oxygen would never make her quit. She keeps a wad of singles in her pocket, and tips every person who helps her. One night she wins eight thousand dollars at the slots, and then comes wheeling into the poker room, where she proceeds to whip everyone at the table. Even the snot-nosed kids are impressed.

Early the next morning she wakes me up and asks me to take her home. My mother is not the kind of person who leaves the casino without trying to give back some of the money she won, so I know something is wrong. I ask her if she's all right, but she just shrugs. In the car she leans her head on the window and falls asleep. A few miles from the house she shares with my sister, Helene, and her husband, Harvey, she wakes up. "I can't go back to the casino again," she says in a little girl's voice. "I can't see a fucking thing anymore." I pull to the side of the road, where we hold each other's hands and stare straight ahead. "You can still play the slots," I offer, but she just shakes her head.

When I call her from Atlantic City, Vegas, or Los Angeles, I tell her all about my exploits. When I lose, we go over what kinds of mistakes I might have made, and how I could play better. Whenever I win, I put some cash in an envelope and send it to her. She uses the money to buy presents for my nieces and nephews, or to tip her healthcare aides. Every day she tells me how proud she is of me, and the unqualified love I hear in her voice is better than any full house I could get.

ELEVEN

Welcome to Paradise

After a few months' hiatus, I go back to the Taj poker room. To my surprise, the room, which had been bursting at the seams for the past year or so, is half empty. I keep asking the dealers what's going on, but no one seems to know. They're too busy bitching about their small tips. Finally a Vietnamese dealer comes to the table. "No players here tonight," she says as she gets settled. "Everyone playing online."

"What's that mean?" I ask.

"Why come to casino when you can stay home and play in pajamas?" she says with a shrug.

The other players don't take notice, but my antennae go up into the stratosphere. I have never heard about online gambling—it's still in its infancy in 1999—but immediately it seems genius, the smartest idea I've ever been privy to. For the next few nights I ask the other players if they've played poker online, but none have. I'm certain I will take a foray into this new world. I'm Columbus, ready to discover, ready to conquer.

As soon as I get back to my office, I start looking up online poker. It takes some time to find the sites—there are only a few. I sign on to one called Paradise Poker, because its logo shows a gorgeous Caribbean beach: blue sky, even bluer water, white sand, one majestic palm tree. It seems like a good omen, as my favorite place to vacation is the Caribbean.

My computer is still on dial-up—cable hasn't come to my town yet—and it takes close to two hours to download their software. I have to register, sign in, and then choose an onscreen name. Sloane, my middle name, which nearly no one knows, feels mysterious. Connected to me, but not really. Am I over eighteen? I check the box, assuring them that I am.

You can play for real cash or for pretend money. They give you two thousand dollars in play money, and you go to one of the tables. I click a little icon, and there Sloane is, sitting at a table. Go figure, I hear my mother say. There is a little dialogue box on the bottom of the screen where players can talk to one another. The game is deadly slow, probably because we're all on dial-up, but after three hours, I have close to three thousand dollars. Okay, it's not real, but I feel like a total winner.

I spend the next few weeks with my pretend money, playing with my virtual friends. I hate the fact that I can't touch the cards, can't see the players, don't know who they really are. But I love that I can do this all day. Problem, though—every time someone phones me, the call takes me offline. I hang up on everyone and hurry back to Paradise. Problem temporarily resolved.

Eventually I have run my pretend bankroll up to eighty thousand chips. It's a little like being in a car without a steering wheel, or the difference between masturbating and having great sex with someone you care about, but I've had a blast. And if I can make *eighty thousand* in a couple of months . . . no, I'm not going to start thinking that way. I know that with pretend money, the betting and play is a lot looser than at a real poker table; after all, no one is losing anything they really care about, except maybe pride. I keep in mind what my goal is here—four to six thousand a month. Maybe just a little more. I can pay all my bills, travel when I want, go see my mother more often. I can buy my sister a fancy new car, get my niece a bigger house. Then I can help everyone I know who doesn't have enough money. I'd never take another job. I could play poker from sunup till sunset. I would be in heaven. Really, who wouldn't?

◆ ◆ ◆

Here's my plan: I will charge three hundred dollars' worth of chips to my credit card. I'll play until I have doubled my money, or for six hours, whichever comes first. After six or seven hours of poker, I start to get batty and do stupid things. At Hollywood Park one night, where I had been for far too many hours, I took my bra off at the table. I didn't lift my shirt over my head, but I did that thing women have been doing since Mary realized that no one was watching and Joseph wouldn't have paid attention to her sagging tits, anyway. I reached my arm around my back to unfasten, slipped one strap out the right sleeve, the other out the left, pulled the bra from under my shirt, and before it was my bet, stuffed it in my handbag. Everybody at the table was staring at me. Tamika, the dealer, said, "Cool," but the look on the faces of the other players told me it was anything but.

Whining and gloating are the other traps I can fall into when I'm cranky, the two things Keith hates most. That's why six hours is my limit. If I lose my original buy-in, I'll turn off the computer and forget about this. Maybe forever, maybe just for a few weeks. If playing for pretend money was like sitting in a stalled car, though, this should be like driving a Corvette on the freeway.

It's a good plan, right? And because I have taught myself to be patient in the casinos, because I have learned to leave when I'm winning, because I feel so confident, it's foolproof.

Obviously, it's time to give Paradise my credit card and start playing for real.

◆ ◆ ◆

It's just nine a.m. when I go to my office, get online, sign into Paradise Poker, and give them my credit card number. Up to this point I had never bought anything online, except for airline tickets, which somehow seemed safe and official. But this turns out to be so quick and easy. Paradise Poker takes a few dollars out of each pot, called the *rake*. The amount of the rake depends on how big the stakes are. They are looking for as many players as they can get here at Paradise. They want me so badly, in fact, that they give me fifty dollars as a sign-up bonus.

The choice is stud or hold'em, at different money levels. I choose a $1/$2 stud table. There are six other players already seated. I take my good luck charms out of my pocket and place them next to my mouse. They con-sist of two pieces of sea glass that I found along the shore in Puerto Rico, and a silver coin from L.A.'s famous card room the Bicycle Club, which I bought at a pawn shop on Melrose Avenue long before I started playing poker. On the head of the coin is the jester holding an ace of clubs. I have had these three talismans in my pocket for years, and cannot remember a poker game I've played without them. The coin is a great thing to put on top of my cards so I can protect them from getting tossed into the muck, and the pieces of sea glass are like New Age rosary beads. I rub them back and forth in my hand, like Captain Queeg right before the mutiny.

My father and uncles had their own lucky charms—shoes, underwear, socks, pants, and shirts. When they'd win, they would take all their clothes off and drape them gingerly over hangers, which would be hooked around the knob of the closet, ready for their next foray to the track or the casino. I can remember Broadway's wife screaming at him because he had been wearing the same clothes every day for almost two months. All she wanted to do was wash them. He wagged his finger at her like Ralph Kramden. "Don'tcha dare," he'd warned. "Those clothes are lucky." When he lost, a few nights later, he tossed them in the hamper, their juju now expired.

My father had carried a small brass coin no bigger than a nickel that he had found on the street years before I was born. It was always in his pocket, and I'd watch him at the track as he rubbed that coin, shining it to a perfect gleam every time. But one night, when a long shot he had bet on pulled up a few lengths before the finish line, fell to the ground, and had to be put down, my father dropped the coin in the garbage can, along with the losing ticket, on our way out of Yonkers. I think about that coin still, wondering how it could have so quickly lost its power.

My poker buddies use baseball caps as their good luck charms. They all wear one to the game, and turn them around when they're not doing well. I start bringing home hats for them from my travels and they pile up in the corner of Michael's house. Hollywood Park Casino. The Taj Mahal. A *Do the Right Thing* hat that Spike Lee gave me when I interviewed him. They ditch their hats and put on one of these when they need a change of luck. For Christmas one year, they buy me a shiny silver tiara, and I place it on my head like a proud princess when I need to change my own juju.

Now I look at my computer screen and wish myself good luck. No, not just in my head—I actually say the words out loud. Talking to myself is nothing new, but I cringe, because when the waiters and the valet guys in Atlantic City wish me luck, I want to put my fingers in my ears and sing so I don't hear them. I hate being wished good luck. It feels like the boogeyman is laughing behind my back, and what he's really saying is, *Bad luck, bad luck, I hope you rot in hell.*

The computer deals my cards and my adrenaline is pumping. This is going to be so much faster than in the casinos, because there won't be any small talk and no dealer screwups. People won't have to look at their cards four or five times, because your cards are staring right at you. This is going to be so quick—in or out, call or fold, yes or no.

In fact, the game is mind-numbingly slow. One player bets, it takes another minute or more for the next player to call or fold, and so on. In the casinos, peer pressure and the dealers keep the game moving. But here it's hard to say if players are slowing the game on purpose or if it's their computers and dial-up screwing with all of us.

Whatever the problem, in the first hour we don't play more than six or seven hands. At the casinos they deal between thirty and forty hands per hour, depending on the game. I am going nuts. Stand, sit, up, down. Read the *New York Post* between bets, dust my desktop, scratch, stretch. At this rate I'll have to play twenty-four hours a day to make some money.

By six at night I only have eighty dollars left. Nine hours and I'm down two hundred and twenty dollars. I'm cross-eyed from staring at the computer all day. I've already violated my first rule: I've played for more hours than I should have. I go home, not sure how to rate this experience. I can't meet Steve's eyes.

The next morning I am back at my office, early. I place my good luck charms next to an enormous bottle of water and sign on. I take my eighty dollars to a hold'em table. Hold'em, by nature, is quicker than stud, so maybe that will move things along.

It sure does—within thirty minutes I have close to three hundred dollars. I take a break and meet Steve for lunch. He wants to sit outside at the café and talk, but I wolf down a sandwich and head back to my office. Busy, busy, busy.

Within an hour, I'm up to five hundred dollars. I sign off, pump my fists in the air, dance around the room.

This is the moment when I should leave—when I'm ahead. Tomorrow is another day. This is when I should realize that everything I hoped for has come to fruition. This is when I should call Steve and tell him we're going out to dinner.

This is not when I should go back to Paradise, get into a higher-stakes game, and lose all my money in an hour. But that's what I do.

I am so surprised that I put another three hundred dollars on my credit card and go back to the same table, where I play smart for a few hours, win a few big hands, and then lose five enormous pots in a row. After the last one, my balance says five dollars. I am sitting in complete shock when the other players start typing like demons in the dialogue box. One of the players writes *what a loser,* and another says *yeah, he played like an idiot.* Another writes *glad you knocked him out,* and the rest write *lol,* with lots of exclamation points. I look at those *lol*s, and my heart sinks. *LOL,* laughing out loud. They are talking about me. They are laughing at me. I am furious, humiliated, and I have just lost more money than I ever have before.

Okay, time out. Calm down. What the fuck is going on? I'm walking in circles around my desk. I finger the pieces of beach glass, take long sips of water, try to figure out what went wrong. I thought I played really smart: I played slow, only played really good hands, didn't get sucked into staying in when I knew I was second best. That was the good news. The bad news was that I couldn't read the other players. I couldn't talk to them, watch their hands, see how they handled their cards or their chips. I couldn't *be* with them.

I have lost before, sure, but never that quickly. And never that anonymously. At a casino, at least I could have stared at the guy who was taking my money. I could judge for myself if the other players were colluding, or if I was the "fish" at this table, the weak player that everyone is out to beat. I've been on both sides, been the fish and the fisherman, and one of the things I'm good at is sussing out who's who. When I first started playing for bigger stakes in the casinos and realized I was the weakest player at the table, I went home and read poker books, dealt out hands. I didn't go back for weeks, until I taught myself to be more aggressive, to not go on tilt when someone drove me crazy, to not listen to the taunts and jibes of the other players. This took some time, but rarely was I ever the fish again.

Whenever I walk into a casino, I know exactly how much I am willing to lose. Whether it's a hundred or five hundred, I never reach into my pocket for more. I have never gone to the ATM machine at a casino, although there are usually dozens of them. And I never break my rule. At my Wednesday-night game, I always start with ninety-nine dollars, and have never lost it all. I'm good about keeping to my budget. When I started winning a lot in the casinos, I kept my cash in my mother's velvet purse. That purse kept getting thicker and thicker.

If I were losing at a casino I would take a walk, relax for half an hour, regroup. I would go to the coffee shop, read the paper, talk to a stranger until I felt the tension leave my body. And when I went back to play I would have been able to make small talk and get to know the other players, however briefly or superficially. I might have decided to change tables, or to leave altogether. But whatever I did, I would not have been laughed at out loud.

I talk myself down, as if I'm a baseball player who has

just made ten errors in a row—I can do better tomorrow; everyone has a bad day; the team is behind me and every-thing will be okay. I shut the computer down and walk out of my office.

◆ ◆ ◆

At home, I make dinner, and then sit in front of the tele-vision, glumly watching an old movie. When Steve comes home and asks how my day went, I shrug. I pretend to listen to what he has to say. I tell him I have a migraine. He brings me ibuprofen, and his concern makes me feel wretched.

I lie in bed, awake. What keeps coming back again and again isn't the fact that I lost all those hundreds of dollars. It's not even that I was laughed at. It's this: they called me *him*. They thought I was a man. In my life no one has ever mistaken me for a man. Part of me is annoyed—I am woman, damn it. And being female has been a great edge at the poker table. Flirting is an integral part of who I am, and it has certainly never hurt me, in life or in poker. And talking to the other players is my secret weapon: they open up, I listen, I intuit things about them that can be used against them later. Most of this happens on a subconscious level, but it has yet to fail me.

The more I think about it, the more my anger shifts

to a feeling of power. I get it. *Him. He* can scare the other players in ways I never could. *He* can write things like *lol*, things I would never do. *He* can probably start winning.

I'm back at my office at seven in the morning. I am going to kick some serious ass today. Actually, *he* is going to do the kicking.

I go to the virtual cashier and try to charge five hundred dollars, but three hundred per day is the limit. I figure with more money, I'll have a better chance. But three hundred it is. I go to a hold'em table, take out the good luck charms, and wait for a good hand. It comes almost immediately—I am dealt a pair of kings. I bet and three other players stay in. The flop is king of spades, ace of diamonds, two of hearts. Unless someone has a pair of aces, I have the best hand. I bet and the other three players still stay. The next card is a four of diamonds. No threat. I bet, but the other three players are still nipping at my heels. The last card is a ten. Of diamonds. Can it be that I will be beat by a diamond flush? Did someone stay in with only one diamond on the flop, hoping to get two more in a row? This would be so stupid as to be impossible, but here in Paradise nothing seems out of the question. I am so unsure of myself that I check. Two other players check, too, but the last player bets. I call. And I'm beaten by a six of diamonds and a jack of diamonds.

Son of a bitch. That's what I type, but it comes out as

Son of a *****, because Paradise Poker is obviously the last bastion of civility. *Motherfucker. Mother*******, it reads. I pick up the phone and throw it across the office. When I look back at the computer screen, there are three *lol*s. Laugh at this, I think, and then I play like a complete idiot until all my money is gone. I retch, go home, and promptly pick a fight with Steve so I can storm into the guest room and cry myself to sleep.

The next day I write until three in the afternoon. I don't go near Paradise, I try not to even think about it. I write. I finish a story about Rebecca De Mornay and send it to my editor. She e-mails back an hour later to tell me that the story is fabulous, she loves it, have a wonderful day. I'm feeling good. So good, in fact, that at four o'clock I sign on to Paradise and charge today's three hundred. Within an hour I have run it up to over six hundred. Okay, all right, I have finally found my rhythm. There will be no stopping me now. I leave the office, thinking all is well in the world.

I lose the six hundred by noon the next day. I charge three hundred more. I lose that, too. The next day is the same. And the next.

In between playing, I scream till my throat is raw. I punch the cushions on the couch. I slam things down. Hard. I curse my own stupidity, the other players, the fact that I know I'm better than this.

At home I'm a moody bitch. Steve begs me to tell him

what's going on, but I cannot. Instead, I convince him that I have a lot on my mind and need some space. When friends ask, I tell them they're imagining things. I hate myself, hate the liar I have become, hate everything and only want to win my money back.

After ten days, when I try to charge another three hundred, I'm told that three thousand dollars per month is the limit they will let me charge. I go nuts. I start hitting my computer screen, yelling that this is my money and no one has the right to tell me what to do with it. I e-mail Paradise Poker to plead my case, but they refuse to up my limit.

Since I can't play poker, I take assignments in New York and Los Angeles. From the outside I seem fine, but inside I am roiling. Could it be that this whole thing is a scam, that somewhere, in Paradise, maybe, there are hundreds of computers, and they are all playing against me?

Can it be that I only understand poker when there are real faces and bodies in front of me, not when they're virtual?

I get a check from *Cosmopolitan*, and pay the rent, phone, and electric bills for my office. I write a check to one credit card company for twelve hundred dollars; write a check to another for nine hundred. At three hundred a day, that's just one week of Paradise payments, I think, sick to my stomach. I have less than sixty dollars left.

♦ ♦ ♦

For months I stick to this routine—charge three hundred a day for ten days, then work the other twenty. I have no money left for anything but essentials. Where's that car I'm going to get for my sister? Where's all the extra time I'll have? I come up with a better plan, much better. I charge three hundred a day for ten days, but I don't play. I just let the money grow in my Paradise account. When I have a bankroll of three thousand, I go to a $10/$20 hold'em game. I get beat by players that are staying in with shit, I get beat by players that are laughing at me. The only common thread is that I get beat. The money doesn't last four days.

I will stop tomorrow, I tell myself. Or Monday. Or the first of the month. Right after I win back what they owe me.

♦ ♦ ♦

I don't stop. Instead, I convince Paradise Poker to up my monthly buy-in to five thousand dollars. I find that it's as easy to lose five hundred a day as it was to lose three.

Please, please, please, I whisper into my pillow. *Please, please, please.* I'm not sure who I'm begging. Certainly not god. From the time I was little I knew that god did not concern himself with gamblers. My uncles were as sure of this as that they'd eat gefilte fish at Passover. They prayed to him, sure, but even *they* felt that god had bigger and better things to do. I'm sure god would *like* to help gamblers—if ever there was a group begging for divine intervention, this was it. Gamblers will agree to anything, ANYTHING, if god will just get both those dice to land on sixes, or give them a jack and an ace at the blackjack table just as they had doubled their bet. But no, god doesn't take an interest in this, I'm sure. Because which of them would he choose? If he picks one pony over the other, or one set of dice, well, you see the havoc that could cause. And anyway, god is apparently too busy working his magic for professional baseball players, who point to the sky and kiss their crosses whenever they hit a home run, make a great catch, or win the game. It's probably the eleventh commandment: *Thou shall help all baseball players, especially the Latinos, but no, not those asinine gamblers. Enough would never be enough for them, anyway.*

Please, please, please, I repeat, until I fall asleep.

◆ ◆ ◆

Here's the one thing I've been addicted to most of my life: cigarettes. I have fought my love for, and disgust of, cigarettes since I was fourteen, when it seemed cool to stand outside my apartment building and hold a cigarette in a way that made me feel like a bad girl. An older bad girl. My mother always said that cigarettes and coffee were her two best friends, and although I'm not an avid coffee drinker, sharing a smoke with my mother was one of our greatest pleasures. We would go out to the terrace of her apartment in Miami and look out over the water, and we would talk and laugh as my mother's Harrah's Casino ashtray filled up with butts. My mother smoked like a grand old dame, making it look glamorous, and even erotic. As she got older and smoking took its toll, my mother still liked to sit outside and blow smoke up toward the sky. She would hold court, tell wonderful stories, while we—her children, grandchildren, friends—sat transfixed. Every memory of my mother has smoke curling up around the edges.

Here are the things I didn't become addicted to: alcohol, Quaaludes, sleeping pills, speed, cocaine, heroin, LSD, Vicodin, Valium, OxyContin. Not that I didn't try. Believe me, I took my share, and yours. And a few other people's. I always said I would try anything at least twice, but the truth is that I took some drugs hundreds of times. When my cousins had money, there was always an abundant supply of cocaine. But listening to people babble till four in the morning never interested me, so I would take a sleeping pill, or two or three, and climb in my bed, where their chatter would get muffled. No drugs ever got to me in that way that twists your insides and makes sanity fly out the window.

I watched my cousins and friends fight their addictions, and when they would disappear for a year or two, or go into rehab, or in one case die, some part of me wouldn't really understand. I was a judgmental bitch, as more than one of them pointed out. I just thought, *Quit, stop already. What's your fucking problem?* I believed in willpower, in mind over matter, in cowboying up.

I've been obsessed, sure—with certain men, with knitting at one point, with my career. But addicted? No. And if I were to get addicted, gambling would have been at the bottom of the list. I saw the heartache it caused some of my aunts, when their husbands were blowing the rent money at the track and would come home with cockamamie stories about how they had lent the money to a friend and would have it back by the end of the month. Or when they would get calls at home from angry bookies and they would pretend that it was a friend, calling to talk. We heard it in the way they would whisper, the way they would walk into another room, the fear in their voices.

My mother, lonely after Aunt Tillie and Uncle Benny died, started going to the casinos in Florida and the Bahamas, and losing too much at the slot machines. She was still working, making a good living, but sometimes she would call me, crying, and admit that she had lost a few hundred more than she could afford. I would take some money out of the velvet purse and send it to her. Using my poker winnings to pay for her gambling losses was an irony that wasn't lost on either of us.

I say it louder—I will stop tomorrow. Monday. Or certainly by the first of the month. But the only thing I hear clearly is the siren song of Paradise.

TWELVE

Hats & Eyeglasses
Redux

I go to $20/$40 hold'em. It's really a no-brainer—this way I will win my money back quicker. I get killed. I go to two-person tables, where I only have one person to beat. I get beat. I go to hold'em, then stud, then back to hold'em. Nothing works.

I barely sleep anymore. I get into bed, get out, read in the living room, walk around the house. Our dog, Buster, starts eyeing me warily—sometimes I literally plop down on the floor beside him and hug him so tight that he can't get any air. Other times I keep him up all night with my pacing. When I finally fall asleep, I wake up in a sweat, scared that everything I cherish is about to evaporate. I become very familiar with three o'clock in the morning, and four.

At the same time I'm throwing money out the window, Steve is wondering if he should spend a hundred dollars on some gears that he wants for a sculpture. Should he buy new tires or ride the old ones until they're bald? Steve is apprehensive about money in the best of times, and he doesn't have a clue that we have entered the worst.

How will he still love me, knowing what a degenerate I am? Why would my friends want to be near someone so out of her mind? I think of running away, but I know that in the computer age, there is no place I can disappear to anymore. I think of suicide, a thought I haven't entertained since I was a teenager. I picture myself in a mental institution, drooling in the corner. Steve and my family are going to be so horrified and disappointed in me when they find out. My friends will shun me. I can't stand the sight of me.

I will stop tomorrow. Or Monday. But definitely by the first of the month.

I'm still getting bounced offline by the phone. I get so annoyed whenever this happens that I come up with a simple plan: I tell all my friends not to bother me at work. I tell my family the same thing. When one of them breaks the rule, I am very impatient and make it clear that I can't be bothered. Busy, busy, busy. They stop calling.

One day I run five dollars up to seventeen hundred. I run the seventeen hundred down to nothing the next day. I play from early morning till dinnertime. I start bringing Chinese food home five nights a week because I can't be bothered cooking.

I don't think things can get worse. And then of course they do. One of our closest friends, Fred, stumbles while walking down the street in Manhattan. By the end of that week he's been diagnosed with brain and lung cancer. We met Fred in the mid-seventies. He was single then, and would have dinner with us a few nights a week. I can remember clearly the day after he met Tory at a friend's wedding, and how infatuated he was. They got married in our house, and we had dinner and Trivial Pursuit nights once a week while their son, Nick, was growing up. Nick is one of the young boys that I taught to play poker.

Fred is smarter than anyone I've ever known. In the middle of graduate school, where he majored in biochemistry, he detoured—first to South America, and then back east, where he became a woodworker instead of a research scientist. His high-end architectural millwork shop is down the road from Steve's. His lifelong dream was to open a barbecue joint, and he never tired of trying to come up with the perfect recipe for ribs. We celebrate every one of Nick's birthdays with him and Tory, know each other's families, and share the same group of close friends. I love spending time with Fred, and the thought that his razor-sharp mind might start to fail is unbearable to me.

I think of this as I play poker. I think of how much worse other people have it than me. I worry about these friends of mine, I worry about myself, about Steve, and what's about to happen to all of us.

I fret about Nick, too. He's going to lose a parent when he is too young to be out in the world by himself. I remember how frightened and angry I was in the years after my father died. I get so melancholy I can hardly function.

But I keep playing.

Stories start to appear about online poker scams. They say that some of the poker sites are rigged against certain players, and that the players who win all the time are really working for the site. I read these stories with enormous interest. If this is true, then there's no chance for someone like me. I have believed since the day I started playing online that the field might not be level, that some players seem to win with really bad cards, while I lose with great ones.

This is way beyond luck. But maybe these stories are written by people like me, people who can't win online. Maybe they're being written by a bunch of bellyaching losers.

I keep playing.

Other stories come out, claiming that oftentimes you are not even playing against real people, that there are computer programs playing for many of the players, and there's no way to beat these programs. The computer makes the right bets, and folds without wondering if it's been beat. It never gets personally involved in the outcome of a hand.

I keep playing.

Fred's illness accelerates quickly, and he starts to fail in a myriad of ways. He keeps going to his shop, but it's getting clearer to everyone that he doesn't have much time left. Right before winter settles in, Fred can no longer leave the house. He's getting weaker and has trouble walking. Although he has what we start to call mental blips, where he loses words or whole trains of thought, most of the time his mind is clear. Tory asks if I'd come to the house during the day and keep him company while she goes to work. I can bring my laptop and work in the living room, or I can just spend time with Fred. She wants to make sure that he's not alone, and that someone is there to give him lunch.

I wish I could say yes without hesitation. I want to be that person, the one who puts other people before herself, and does it with grace and style.

And I do say yes, of course I do. But it's not easy, and not because I don't want to care for Fred and be with him.

How the hell am I going to win back all that money if I'm away from my office? How am I going to beat the odds, beat the house, beat fucking Paradise Poker? How?

For the next five or six weeks, Fred and I fall into a comfortable routine. I come over around ten each morning. Tory shows me the lunch options in the fridge, reminding me what time Fred has to take his medications. She leaves, and if I'm not on deadline, I crawl on top of the quilt next to Fred and nap. It's the only dreamless, worriless sleep I have had in over a year. When I wake, Fred is reading *The New York Times*. He always smiles down at me, as if my snoring is a magnificent song that he has been longing to hear. I make us lunch, and then he reads to me from the science or business sections. He explains string theory, and quantum physics. He makes me understand about how ducks imprint on their mothers, and what a 401(k) actually does. Then he does the *Times* crossword in pen. When he falls asleep after lunch, I read the *New York Post* and do the easy crossword puzzle in the back.

As Fred gets sicker, he stops reading his beloved *Times*. I start reading the *Post*'s gossip section, Page Six, aloud to him, getting him interested in who is sleeping with Puff Daddy, what Jennifer Lopez wore to this opening or that one. We read the blind items about who is cheating on their spouse, or who is bulimic, or which actor is secretly gay. He asks lots of questions, and laughs a full belly laugh when I tell him which celebrities I think these stories are about. Fred has never been concerned with pop culture, which is why we were the unbeatable Trivial Pursuit team—I knew movies and sports, and he knew everything else. But in those last few weeks, he smiles his shy little grin and listens raptly while I explain entire plots of television shows he has never seen. I tell him about going to Yankee Stadium when I was a kid, about how safe and great that neighborhood was back in those days. I read him my celebrity interviews, stories he would never have read, and he tells me how much he enjoys them. I'm delighted, although I do realize that he's my captive audience.

Fred's brother and other friends come to visit, and I make endless pots of coffee, bring plates of sandwiches and cookies, and leave them alone so they can be with him. At night, Tory and I make simple dinners, and Steve joins us around Fred's bed. Fred's parents, Emma and Tom, come to see him every other day, carting loads of food and supplies, as if we are battening down for war. The child of Russian Jews, Emma is still waiting for the Cossacks to bang down the door. There will never be enough toilet paper or tinfoil in the house to make her feel safe. Emma and Tom are generous, wonderful people who are completely distraught at the prospect of watching their firstborn die. When they leave one afternoon, Fred is exhausted. He isn't talking a lot that day, as if just forming thoughts takes all his energy. I ask him if he wants to go to sleep, but he shakes his head, no. He pats the bed next to him, and I flop down on it. We lay there in silence for a while, until he says, "Tell me a story."

I turn toward him. Our faces are just inches apart. "Okay," I whisper. "I've been playing poker online."

Fred arches his eyebrows. "Go on."

"I'm getting killed. I'm hemorrhaging money. Everything that makes me a good player in the real world is completely useless online. I know I should never do it again, but I've gone completely crazy. I can't stop. I'm so pissed at them for taking all this money from me that all I think about is winning it back. Nobody knows." Both my voice and my body are quivering, but I will not cry. Fred has enough on his plate. I'm holding my breath.

Fred looks at me, and I can see compassion and confusion in his face. "Well, now *I* know," he finally says, reaching for my hand and rubbing it with his. I exhale. We don't speak. My terror recedes a bit in our silent language. Within minutes we are both sound asleep.

Fred dies two weeks later. Steve and I are with Tory and Nick when it happens—we've been sleeping at their house for a couple of nights by then—and we are all bowled over to see that everything that had made him "Fred" disappears with his last breath.

Fred's body is cremated.

My secret has literally gone up in smoke.

If this were a Hollywood movie, this would be the big turning point, the climax, the part where I come to my senses and stop playing poker online. The orchestra would cue up a song of redemption and hope. There would be a collective sigh of relief. Everything would work out for everyone, including all the minor players.

But this isn't a Hollywood movie.

♦ ♦ ♦

A few weeks later, in the darkest part of that winter, when the sun is too weak to warm me and snow covers every surface, I return to Paradise.

Things do not improve.

Steve and my friends continue to ask what's the matter with me. Some days I am frantic and ready to scream; other times, lethargic and depressed. I stop calling people to see how they are, stop taking their calls. Everyone is so worried. When they do get through to me, I tell them that they're mistaken, that I am fine. But I know they see me sinking, the hats and eyeglasses floating up.

I can't imagine what will make me stop, what will derail the runaway train that my life has become.

I'll stop tomorrow. Monday. First of the month.

One day my phone rings and bounces me offline. I

slam my hand on my desk, jerk the phone to my ear, and say, "Hello?" with such contempt that whoever is on the other end will surely know they have interrupted me.

"Cookie?" my mother says, and I can hear how tentative and unsure she sounds.

"What's up?" I say, waving my hand in a circle, *hurry up, get to the point, busy, busy, busy.*

My mother doesn't answer.

"What?" I say, no less stridently.

And then I hear an intake of air and a little gurgle, as if she is being strangled.

I turn away from the computer screen. "Mommy?" I ask, concern mounting. "Are you okay?"

"No," she says.

I stand up. My heart's pounding. "Who's there?" I have a horrible vision of my mother being hurt. In Miami, right after the Mariel Boat Lift, when Castro had emptied his prisons and insane asylums and shipped the whole lot of them off to south Florida, my five-foot-one, hundred-and-twenty-pound mother was attacked by a six-foot-four monster with prison tattoos all over his fingers. In Spanish, he shouted at her while he grabbed her arm. In English, she told him to fuck off. He pulled her purse off her shoulder and then took hold of the gold chains around her neck. She struggled—one of the chains held an antique coin that had been a present from my father. She had worn it every single day since he died. The robber was evidently not a sentimental sort—he punched her square in the face, knocking her down in the parking lot. "I fell onto Daddy's coin," she managed the next morning through her bruised jaw, now wired shut. "No way was I letting him get that."

The memory is more than I can bear.

"Mommy?" I scream now. "Who's there? Can you hear me?"

"Of course I can hear you," she says. "I'm blind, not deaf."

"Is someone in the house with you?"

"Just Meg," she says, referring to the healthcare aide who comes in for a few hours every day to help my mother shower and dress.

"Are you in trouble?" I ask.

"Are you?"

I sit down again. "What?"

"Are you in trouble?"

"Why do you ask?" I say, trying to calm down. And then my mother, who hasn't cried in over forty years, who swears that if the floodgates finally reopen there will be no way to close them again, begins to sob.

"What is it?" I ask, frightened in a different way now. "Talk to me. Please. Why are you crying?"

"Because I'm not sure what I did to you," she says through her tears.

"You didn't do anything. I don't even know what you're talking about." The thought goes through my head that my mother has become senile overnight. "Calm down," I beg. "Tell me what's going on."

Five minutes pass until she can speak in her normal voice. "I want to know if I did something wrong," she finally says.

"No, of course not."

"Then why are you so mad at me?"

I don't know what she's talking about.

"For the last year or so, whenever I call, you're too busy to talk," she says sadly. "You're short-tempered with me. You don't call like you used to, we don't talk the way we always did. When you come to visit you seem like you're a million miles away. I know I must have done something, something very bad, to make you this angry. But I swear, I don't know what it is." She starts crying again.

I put my head down on the desk. I want to reassure her, but I can't do it in this place I've made my hell. "Let me go home and call you," I finally say. "Have Meg wash your face with a cool washcloth, okay?

"Okay," she says.

"Promise me you'll calm down. I'll be home in ten minutes. Please, you didn't do anything. Just believe me."

I turn off the computer and drive the six miles to my house as fast as Mario Andretti. I call before my coat's even off. There's a part of me that thinks I might tell her the whole story—I have rarely left anything out with her. She knew about the drugs and the boys and all the other dirty little details of my life. And telling her would be such a relief.

But she is old. She's experienced too much sadness, and I can't be the cause of more.

"Listen to me," I say when she answers. "You're right that I haven't been myself for a while. But the truth is, it has nothing to do with you. Something's happening to me, and I can't explain it, even to you. Not until I resolve it."

We talk for over two hours, trying to catch our breath. I don't tell her about Paradise. Instead, I think back to all the stories my mother loves and start telling them. I remind her of how, when I was young, I would make her wear her flimsiest dress to her Weight Watchers meetings, because Keith and I and the other cousins would bet nickels and dimes on which of our mothers would lose the most, and I didn't want an extra half-pound of clothing to ruin my chances.

"I went to those meetings looking like a whore," she says, although she pronounces it WHO-er, rhyming it with *sewer*, the way we used to back in the Bronx.

I reminded her of when my father would throw quarters to the bottom of the pool at the bungalow colony, and how Keith and I would push each other and try to be the first to get them. "Remember how my eardrum burst that time and I kept going to the bottom, and Keith started crying because he could see the blood and I wouldn't come up for air?"

"You two," she says.

"Remember when I was in Mrs. Hewitt's second-grade class?" I asked. "Remember how she made us all stand up and tell the class what our parents did for a living? I stood up and proudly said, 'My dad's a CPA, and my mom is a bookie.'"

The other seven-year-olds had looked back at me, blankly. Mrs. Hewitt asked them if they knew what a CPA was, and they all shook their heads, no.

"It's someone who does a lot of things with numbers," I told them. "And a bookie . . ."

Mrs. Hewitt clapped her hands. "Enough of that," she said crossly.

My parents were called into school that afternoon, and my mother had to explain to Mrs. Hewitt that she was a book*keeper*, not a book*maker*. This was the story that my mother and I told each other over and over, the one that was sure to make us laugh until we cried. But our tears were too close to the surface, and a chuckle was all she could manage.

Gambling was the currency that my mother and I used with each other; it was, along with her family and good food, the thing she loved most in this world. It was usually enough to make her happy. But not today.

"Please don't worry anymore," I begged.

"I'll stop worrying about you when I die," she said. "You're my baby."

By the time we hung up, I had convinced her that whatever had been happening to me was over, that I was going to be okay.

Now I just had to convince myself.

THIRTEEN

Help

In the early 1990s I became friends with a good-looking, notorious character actor whom I'll call Tony Arthur. He was old-fashioned in a lot of ways: courteous, well dressed, generous to a fault. He was also obnoxious in one particular way: he couldn't be trusted around any of my women friends, because he was sure to grab a breast or an ass. I had to slap him across the face a couple of times until we came to an understanding. A truce, of sorts.

Everywhere we went people recognized him, and he would stop and talk to each and every one of them, signing autographs and telling stories about the directors and stars he had worked with, the great independent movies he had been in. I have never seen anyone work a room quite the way he did.

By the time I met Tony he had been clean and sober for a few years. But the stories about his drugging and alcohol abuse were the stuff of legends, always ending with him as the last man standing. He snorted lines with rock stars and actors, groupies and writers. Unfortunately he also shared his stash with his teenage son. They had been strung out on crack for a while when Tony got busted and went to prison. During Tony's incarceration, they both got clean, and when I went to Los Angeles I would go with them to Sunday-morning AA meetings.

These meetings were like a great Sunday brunch: the room was huge and full of sunlight; delicious pastries and three kinds of strong, scented coffees were available in the back of the room. There were over a hundred people at the first meeting I attended. After lots of air kisses, everyone finally got settled, and then an infamous actor strode to the podium, introduced himself, and said he was an alcoholic. Everyone said hello back to him. No one seemed to think it was strange that he had given his full name—obviously no one here cared about the *Anonymous* part of AA. He talked about the films he had been in, and about his famous family. Then he got around to the drugs and drink that had made him so outrageous that he couldn't get work anymore. He told stories about drugs I had never heard of, making them sound so interesting that I wished there had been piles of them, right next to the scones in the back of the room. His voice was melodious and perfectly pitched, and I wished I could write a film to showcase his talent. I could already see him thanking me when he accepted his Academy Award.

He handed the mike to Tony, who talked about directors who had turned him down for parts, and why the actors who got the parts instead weren't remotely as good as he would have been. He mentioned the actors by name. He made jokes about the casting directors who wouldn't touch him anymore, and the crowd roared with knowing laughter. Others got up and told hilarious stories, making alcohol and drug abuse sound like part of a funny script.

The women wore Armani and Manolo Blahniks. Their makeup was flawless. Not a strand of hair was out of place. They were all beautiful, movie-star svelte, and really magnetic. After the Serenity Prayer, people stood around for hours, exchanging cards, slipping each other scripts, making plans for dinner.

It made me wish I was a recovering addict.

I thought about this the morning I finally called Gamblers Anonymous. I had reached bottom, my personal low as they say in recovery lingo, and needed help.

A man answered the phone. "This is Ned," he said.

"Ned," I said, "I have a problem."

"Are you gambling?"

"Yes," I admitted.

"Does your family know?" Ned asked. He sounded completely bored and preoccupied, as if he was clipping his nails and having trouble with those pesky cuticles.

"No, no. No one knows."

"Are you losing more money than you can afford?"

I imagined fat cats in Costa Rica, where Paradise Poker is based, going out to dinner on my money, laughing at me while skanky little hookers in gauzy skirts and see-through halter tops lit their cigars. I saw a gargantuan stack of poker chips, built like the most intricate sand castle, and I watched it get wiped away by a wave. I thought of how that money was gone, gone, gone. I thought of my credit card bills, stacking up like planes at LaGuardia. And how I would have to finally come clean to Steve. This is when I finally lost it—the enormity of all that money, the lying, the fear. I became hysterical. I was wiping gobs of snot from my cheeks and chin.

"Yes," I answered.

"Where do you live?"

I told him.

"Hold on," he said, and then he went away, probably to get those nails buffed.

He was gone for what seemed an eternity. "Hmmm,"

he said when he finally came back. "Don't seem to be any meetings in your area."

"How's that possible?" I said. "Please help me." I was so sure they would have an answer for me that I hadn't considered the alternative.

Nothing.

"Are you there?" I said after a minute.

"Yup."

"Well, what do I do now?"

"Lady, give me your address. I'll send you a packet of info."

I gave him my address, spelling out the name of my town as if we were in the military: *B as in Bravo, O as in Oscar, India, Charlie . . .* I wanted him to get it right. As soon as I finished I heard him hang up.

◆ ◆ ◆

I waited a week. And then another. In the morning I was the first person at my post office, and late in the day, the last. I poured through my mail in a frenzy, waiting to see the Gamblers Anonymous logo. Nothing came.

I didn't want to turn on my computer and be tempted, as if my particular Gateway on my particular desk could send me down the rabbit hole. Instead, I cleaned my office.

I painted the walls. I rearranged the photos and carted out bags of papers that I no longer needed. I changed the position of my desk so it wouldn't feel the way it did when I was playing poker. I waited.

I went to Steve's shop and did filing that had been piling up for decades. I threw out old catalogues. I cleaned my closets. I waited.

I went to Baltimore for a couple of weeks to spend time with my family. My sister, Helene, and brother-in-law, Harvey, could see that I was on the verge of hysteria but didn't know what to do for me. Every day my mother, totally blind now, would say, "Want to tell me what happened?" I didn't answer. I would reach out and hold her hand while tears streamed down my face. It was nice to just sit in her room and watch old movies, talking about Susan Hayward and Barbara Stanwyck as if they were old friends of hers. At night I would make complex, involved gourmet dinners for everyone. I would chop and dice and sauté and braise and roast. I would cook till I was soaked in sweat. My niece, Mara, would bring her young son, Alex, and they would join Helene and Harvey and my mother and me at the table. I would pretend that I was the way I used to be, that everything would realign itself, shift back to a world I understood. I didn't really believe it, but I am well versed in pretending.

Chris and Annie Flanders called and asked Steve and

me to meet them at their amazing oceanfront home in Puerto Rico. I told Annie that I had no money, and she insisted on sending us two plane tickets. Sitting on a deserted white-sand beach, I looked out at the blue sky and that bluest of water and a lone palm tree, and I realized that I was in paradise. Real paradise. When we got home, it became clear to me that Ned wasn't sending that package. Maybe he didn't think I was good enough for Gamblers Anonymous. I had reached out to them, and they had swatted my hand away.

In Los Angeles a few weeks later, I sought out a Gamblers Anonymous meeting about fifteen miles east of Hollywood. I doubted I would run into anyone I knew there, and I needed to see what they had to say.

From the minute I pulled up, it was clear to me that recovering addicts and drunks are having a much better time than recovering gamblers. The church where the meeting was being held looked worn and abandoned. A few men congregated outside, smoking their last cigarette before they went inside. These might have been the only Californians who had never seen the sun. No one had bothered to change out of their sweatpants. Sallow was the color of the day. There were six of us, and I was the only woman. We filed into the room, and two men got busy making a pot of coffee, with water the color of a battleship. Not a scone in sight. We sat down at a long wooden table, chipped like the walls. We introduced ourselves. When the first guy said, "Hi, I'm Bobby Dee," I put out my hand and said, "Hi, Martha Frankel."

"No last names," they shouted at once. I realized that Bobby's last name, at least in this room, was just "D." Four of the men were friends, at least Gamblers Anonymous compatriots. Another guy, like me, was a newcomer. Just as we were repeating our names, some kids came in and said that Father Frank had promised them this room for the night. They were going to be practicing a dance routine. "Are you leaving soon?" they asked.

Bill, the leader, suggested a restaurant down the block. There we found a big, secluded table in the back. We sat down again and ordered coffee from the waitress. There was a lot of talk about whether we should bring out the Big Book, or even the little one. I had no idea what either of these might be. Some of the members wanted to go through the steps, while others were concerned that in public, we should just talk and not draw attention to ourselves. The other newcomer and I had no opinion.

Finally our leader read a short prayer from one of the books, asking a higher power to watch over us and not let us give in to our temptations. He took a newspaper article out of his pocket and read that to us, too. It was about how sick thinking could make people do stupid things. And then he said that whoever wanted to start should just go ahead.

Jim, wearing a worn leather coat with holes in the pockets, had been in GA for over eight years, but had started playing the horses again, and now was a few days short of ninety days clean. Not encouraging.

Tommy stopped tapping his stained fingernails against the table long enough to tell us about his compulsive sports betting, and how he had lost all his money betting Gonzaga to go all the way in the NCAA basketball finals. I had to hold my tongue—I wanted to tell him that only a moron would have bet on Gonzaga. Tommy had been coming to GA for over a decade, but said he had bet on sports that very weekend. This isn't what I want to hear— I'm looking for cure, not remission.

Bobby talked about how he bet on baseball and basketball and football every day for years, until he couldn't pay the bookies and they stopped taking his action. "My wife woke me up at six one morning to say that some guy was leaning against my car, drinking a Heineken. I knew exactly who he was. I went outside and told him that breaking my legs wasn't going to get him his money, and right before he spit on my shoes, he told me that I had a week to pay him." Bobby had to ask his father-in-law to pay off his debts. He had missed every one of his kid's birthday parties, and his family had given up on him.

Mark, the new guy, spent his entire paycheck on scratch-off lottery tickets. Some of the other guys nodded, recounting their own insane lottery horror stories.

Bill had been in the program for over twelve years, but four years before, on a trip to the Jersey shore, he had taken a detour to Atlantic City, and gone on a seven-day bender. His real addiction was sports betting, although he wasn't averse to playing roulette or blackjack. When he came back, having not called home for the whole week, his wife told him she was leaving. She was fed up. "The bitch gives my ten- and twelve-year-old kids scratch-off tickets for their birthdays every year," he said. "Doesn't she understand this addiction?" The vein in his temple throbbed.

I am sitting around a table, talking sports with five men. How familiar is this? I want to take a deck of cards out of my bag and start dealing. Why else would I be here with these losers? Every one of them seemed pathetic. But then they all look at me. "You don't have to share if you don't want to," Bill says, reminding me that I'm one of them.

I take a deep breath. I have never said this to anyone but Fred. "I started playing poker online," I whisper. "And I couldn't stop."

They're waiting for more. But that's the extent of what I can manage right now.

Tommy asks Bill if he can cross-talk and Bill says it's fine. "When was the last time you played?" Tommy asks.

"A couple of months ago," I say offhandedly, although

I know for a fact that it's been sixty-three days since I last signed on to Paradise. Sixty-three. Not one more, not one less.

"What made you stop?"

Have I stopped? It feels more like a hiatus, a little vacation from Paradise. I don't answer.

"Do you go on the Internet?" Tommy asks.

I hesitate—I go on the Internet every day to read my e-mail and do research. "You mean to gamble?"

"No," he says, and it's clear that he's annoyed with me. "Do you go on the Internet at all?"

"Sure. I'm a writer and I can't really do my work without—"

"And you haven't gambled at all in a couple of months?"

"No, I haven't," I said, feeling air rushing in instead of out. "I mean, I still play poker with my buddies every Wednesday, but that's not a problem . . ."

Tommy looks like I've thrown ice water in his face. I heard his intake of breath. I might as well have said, *Come on over to my house, Tommy, and we'll bet on the Yankees, shoot some craps, and do some scratch-off lottery tickets. Stay around for a card game, why don'tcha? It'll be a ball!* Tommy snaps. "Addiction isn't a fucking Chinese menu," he hisses. "You can't chose two from column A and none from column B. You have to stop altogether. Second of all, you'll never be able to stay away from gambling if you go on the Internet. You're gonna relapse." He slams his hand on the table to make his point.

Bill asks him to calm down. Tommy apologizes. I don't speak again. I listen for the next hour, until I can't stand hearing one more story about one more horse that slowed down, or one more basketball player who missed an easy layup, or one more pitcher who fell apart in the ninth inning. I stand up, thank them all, and wish them good luck. A little screech escapes me—wishing a table full of compulsive gamblers *good luck* does not seem smart. I practically run to my car. I feel better, superior. And worse, frighteningly inferior.

In college I had a brilliant literature professor, a glum man who was a compulsive eater. He was very honest about his compulsion, although at 350 pounds it wasn't necessary to be. "I can't stop eating," he acknowledged once, when we were sitting in his office, discussing a story I had written.

"When I get home at night, I make three huge dinners. I eat dozens of ice-cream sandwiches. I stuff potato chips in my mouth till I can't breathe. I buy four boxes of Mallomars a day," he confessed. He picked up a paw-ful of M&M's, and shoved them into his mouth.

I didn't know what to say, or why he was telling me this. We had never talked about anything more personal than D. H. Lawrence. A few nights later he had a massive coronary. I went to see him in the hospital that weekend.

"My doctor says I have to go on a diet and start exercising," he told me, looking oddly happy.

He didn't come back to school that year, but when he showed up the next September he was a different man, thinner and walking with a purposeful gait. By the time spring came around, *he* was turned around—literally half the size he had been, and full of good humor. He started dating a cute history professor, and I often saw them out on their bicycles, sweat glistening on their faces.

He took me to lunch one day, and while we looked at the menu, he confessed that he'd had a premonition that he would have that heart attack.

"If you knew, why didn't you stop eating so much?"

"Shame," he said. "I needed to be shamed." He ate half of what was on his plate, then asked the waitress to wrap the rest. He held up the bag. "For dinner."

Shame. I wonder what would have happened if Fred had been judgmental with me, if he had told me that he thought I was a miscreant, if he had shown derision or scorn. Or if he hadn't touched my hand that day, and through it, my heart. What if he had tried to talk me into stopping?

What if my mother had turned her back on me, knowing that I had done something wrong, even if she didn't know what it was, or how bad it might be? What if she didn't keep telling me how much she loved me, that I could do no wrong in her eyes?

But they didn't turn away from me. In fact, they had pulled me closer, and what they were saying was, *We love you. We're sorry you're in trouble, but we are all failed humans. Welcome to the club.*

They loved me, knowing I might not deserve it—loved me especially if I didn't.

At the time, I hadn't really appreciated what my professor meant, but now I understood it in every fiber of my body.

Soon after my father died, when you might still catch a whiff of his Old Spice and his cigars in little corners of the apartment, my mother and I sat in the kitchen, having dinner. She was wearing a half-slip pulled up above her breasts, and I was, too. She was talking to me as I read the *Post.* I held the paper up in front of me, so she couldn't see my face. I heard what she was saying—something about dinner with my sister that weekend—but I wouldn't acknowledge her. Our lives seemed at an impasse, with her turning toward me, and me turning away. She kept talking, I kept ignoring. I heard the familiar *click* of her Zippo, expected to smell the first hint of her cigarette. Instead she leaned over and lit my newspaper on fire. I jumped up and ran with it to the sink. Flames were shooting above my head. I threw the paper down and ran water over it. Soot flew all around the kitchen. I looked back at my mother with pure loathing. She stared right back. "I know you wish it was me who had died," she said as she did light a cigarette. "And sometimes, God forgive me, I wish it had been you. But this is the way it worked out. It's you and me forever, Cookie. You and me. And don't you ever forget it." She got up and walked out of the room.

I *had* forgotten, and that was my shame. Listening to her anguish on the phone that day, knowing that I had let her down, knowing that it was she who kept me tethered to this earth, was enough to gently tug my heart and wake me up from the trance, the stubborn pull of Paradise.

I sat before my computer for an entire week until I finally hit the DELETE button, banishing Paradise Poker. I felt slaphappy. I blocked them from sending me e-mails, because I was afraid they would start offering me money to come back.

I made dinner at home every night, reconnecting with Steve, who still didn't know what I had been doing, but only that I had slipped away. And that I was returning. We would watch movies, and I'd laugh, realizing that I wasn't holding my breath anymore. Those laughs were lighter than feathers, as if angels were playing in my hair.

I finally admitted to Randy that I wasn't going to write that screenplay. He was disappointed, and tried to talk me back into it. When I said I had had enough of poker, he suggested other scams. He said it would be fun. But I knew better.

I started inviting people over for dinner again, and while I often got quiet or listened as if there were cotton balls in my ears, I was happy to be surrounded by the people I loved, and who loved me back.

And I worked. I took every job I could get my hands on, and bought myself nothing with the money I made. I was paying my penance. I interviewed young actors I had never heard of, and made them sound fantastic. I paid off those credit card bills one by one, then cut them into little bitty shards and threw them in the trash. I tried not to think of the new car I could be driving, the years of mortgage payments I could have made, or that trip to Africa that Steve had his heart set on. I just did my penance, no complaining.

Sometimes, just when I convinced myself that everything was all right, when I felt that I had dodged a bullet and didn't have to worry about getting shot anymore, I would find myself online, looking up Paradise Poker. It was as if I had no control over my hand. When their logo would appear, I'd start to breathe in ragged little gasps. I'd stare at the blue, blue water until I was dizzy. I would yearn for that majestic palm tree so palpably that I could feel sweat forming on my forehead. My finger would hover right above the mouse while I debated if I should hit DOWNLOAD. Maybe just one more time, one more crack at changing my luck. Maybe, maybe, maybe.

But I didn't do it. I remembered the self-loathing, the fear that accompanied Paradise. And I remembered the shame. Slowly, little by little, I felt the vulture's talons, which had held me captive, begin to withdraw from my neck.

Around that time a woman called and told me that she had heard me on the radio, talking about the Academy Awards. "I'm a personal trainer," Dorothy said, "and I'd like to start training you." I was suspicious, but Dorothy was very honest. "I'm new to the area," she told me, "and I have a feeling that if I train you well, you'll fill my gym with your cool friends."

I laughed. I was fifty years old, out of shape, and not remotely interested. I tried to blow her off, but she was determined.

"Let me come to your office and we'll see how it goes. No charge."

She came the next day, bringing along an exercise ball and some free weights. She held the ball against the wall, and told me to lean on it. "Now lower yourself as far as you can," she instructed.

I leaned against the ball and fell right to the floor.

Within a month, I could do twenty squats. Within

a year, I could do fifty, while holding thirty pounds of weight on my shoulders. She had me do crunches till I was ready to vomit, and then made me do thirty more. She told me that if you did them while contracting your pelvic muscles, it felt a little like an orgasm. Not really, but still, my stomach got flat as a board. If I worked my way up to twenty lunges, Dorothy would make me do another five. If I was struggling to press forty pounds, she would add another ten. She was punishing, single-minded, and relentless. She was exactly what I needed.

FOURTEEN

Redemption

My mother became less mobile, hardly ever leaving her bedroom. When I visited I'd make her tell me stories, the ones I had heard a thousand times before, so I could remember them. *Her* memory was as sharp as ever. "A woman we met in the army got married at this old shore club out on Long Island," she told me one day. "It was supposed to be an outdoor wedding, but it poured, so everyone was huddled together in the tent. There was a great band, though, and a small wooden dance floor. You know Daddy, how he loved to dance. We did the Peabody, and the Cha-Cha. It was such a great night." She paused for a minute. "Why was I telling you this? Oh, right— they served lobster Newburgh. We'd never had it before, and Daddy went wild for it. I learned to make it by trial and error, because I couldn't find the recipe in a book. I made it dozens of times before I got it right. It became my signature dish." I closed my eyes, and could smell the sherry.

I spent a week with her and will never forget that when I said "good-bye," she turned and said, "We don't say 'good-bye,' we say 'so long.'" I kissed her again. "So long," I repeated.

Two weeks later she lapsed into a coma.

"Come soon," my sister Helene whispered on the phone that night. "Mommy's waiting for you."

If I knew anything, it was that my mother would never die with me in the room. I'm her baby, and she would never do that to me. But I didn't tell Helene.

I arrived in Baltimore early the next morning. Helene and I fell into each other's arms. From the minute my father died, we had been vigilantly watching my mother, waiting for the other shoe to drop, as they say. But she had outlived all of her friends and everyone in her family, and a part of us just didn't believe that she would ever die.

She'd been living with Helene and Harvey for over ten years by then, and their lives revolved around her. They loved having her with them, and she loved it there, too. She was thrilled that her great-grandson was with them all the time. Alex had no idea that his Gram was blind.

He would cut her meat for her, and hand her the fork, but she did everything else by herself, and was such a creature of habit that her drink was always placed *just so* on the table, her tissues *right there*. He thought helping her with her food was just something you did for old people. Oftentimes *we* would forget that she couldn't see anymore. The television was always on as they ate, and Alex told her all about *Jimmy Neutron, Pokémon,* and *The Simpsons.* "Does Homer Simpson really work in a nuclear power plant?" she asked me one morning. I assured her that he did. She burst out laughing.

Harvey was sitting with my mother when we got back to the house, talking softly and rubbing her hands. I stood out in the hallway and watched him for a moment, this man who treated my mother like a precious jewel. He came out when he saw me, held me tight, and told me that nothing had changed, that she was still breathing and in a coma. He and Helene stood back while I went in to see her.

By the time I walked the seven steps to her bed, my mother had died. I leaned down and kissed her, put my head on her chest and listened. Nothing. I glanced up at Helene and Harvey, who had moved even further back in the hallway to give me more privacy. I didn't want to be the one to tell them, so I continued to kiss my mother, closed her eyes and mouth, whispered softly in her ear. *So long, so long, so long.* She smelled delicious, like the Shalimar she wore every day. I sniffed her neck till I heard Helene and Harvey come back in the bedroom.

Later that day, after all the grandchildren and great-grandchildren had a chance to say good-bye, the funeral director came for my mother's body. As Helene handed him a folder with my mother's burial information, a sheet of paper fell to the floor. Helene and Mara and I all stared at it—it had the familiar butterflies of my mother's stationery, *from the desk of Sylvia Frankel* in raised letters across the top. We three froze. It was a good minute before my sister picked it up and read it to us. *"If you're reading this I'm dead . . ."* it began. *"I want a very simple graveside service and a plain pine box. You don't have to spend a fortune on a coffin to prove to everyone how much you loved me. You proved that to me every day of my life. Love you, Mommy."*

We were dumbstruck. Even dead she was giving orders. We did not call her The General for nothing. Later that night we sorted through her jewelry, took some of her clothing, and opened her wallet. There was $84 in it, and Helene and I each took our $42. "What are you going to do with yours?" my sister asked, only half-kidding.

On a trip to L.A. a month later, I booked a flight that would go through Vegas for a night. I thought of how much my mother loved it there, all the hoopla and yelling, and how she'd make friends with whoever sat next to her at the buffet.

I kept my own money in my left pocket, my mother's $42 in the right. If I used her money at the poker table, I could make it into something. But I decided to be true to her and only played roulette and slot machines, two things I had never tried. I took $20 for the roulette tables at the Mirage and played her numbers—28, 0, and 00. Nothing. I took $5 and put it into the slots. Lost it. Another five there. Nada. It seemed I was on the verge of losing all my mother's money, just the way she almost always did.

Then I remembered something she told me—that the airport slot machines pay the biggest returns in Vegas, because they want you to hear all the screaming when you get off the plane. In the morning I went to the airport, and put that last twelve dollars into a twenty-five-cent Triple Diamond slot machine. These were her favorite. I pulled the lever, and three diamonds came up. I won twenty dollars. I pulled again. I won another twenty. I turned to the man next to me and said, "This is great, huh?" He gave me a withering look. I played for an hour, and ran that twelve dollars up to $208. And that's when I heard the announcement that my plane was leaving. I had to take a paper credit slip from the slot machine and go find a cashier. By the time I ran to my gate they had closed the doors, but I convinced the stewardess to open them and let me on the plane. I think I might have used the words *dead mother*. As I rushed down the aisle, everyone was giving me dirty looks, but I didn't care. I got settled and took my mother's money out of my pocket. Two hundred and eight dollars. It felt like a fortune. I folded it in half and put it in the red velvet purse.

The Address of Paradise Has Changed

A year passed. Then another. The word *paradise* no longer made me want to fall to my knees. I stopped wincing when characters on *The Sopranos* mentioned gambling. Somehow the mania that had held me hostage faded—the way you can someday forget the feel of a favorite lover's tongue on your neck.

◆ ◆ ◆

In 2003, an accountant from Tennessee with the unlikely name of Chris Moneymaker entered an online poker tournament. His buy-in cost him $39. He beat eighteen other players, and was given a seat at another online tournament, this one with sixty players. He won that tournament, too, and was given a coveted $10,000 seat at the World Series of Poker, which had always been a Las Vegas landmark, if almost unknown to the outside world. That year it was covered on national television for the first time. Money-maker went on to win, cashing a check for more than two and a half million dollars. It was his first live tournament. His win opened the floodgates of online poker—there are now hundreds of poker sites, plus hundreds of thousands of online gambling sites, where you can play anything from slots to roulette to blackjack.

Online poker is the fastest-growing segment of the Internet gaming industry. I know this because my fax machine fills up with solicitations from companies that want me to invest with them. Hundreds of thousands of people play poker, slots, blackjack, and roulette online every day. Once again, I was way ahead of my time.

You can now watch poker on television around the clock. This year's WSOP had over six thousand entrants. The payoff for first place was over eight million dollars.

◆ ◆ ◆

On a trip to L.A., I ran into a woman I hadn't seen for a couple of years at the Coffee Bean on Sunset. Her son, a crack and methamphetamine addict, had recently gone to prison for stealing a car. A mutual friend had called to tell me the news.

"How's Paulie doing?" I asked as we sat down at a table outside with our pastries. I had always liked her family and didn't want to ignore the elephant in the room.

"It wasn't his fault," she began, and I thought about how heartsick it makes a mother when their child spins out of control. I was happy that I had never told my mother about Paradise, that I hadn't put her in the position of defending me against myself.

I listened to this mother's pain. Everyone was to blame for Paulie's problems, everyone but Paulie. The car wasn't stolen, just borrowed from a crazy friend, who got mad at Paulie and called the cops. The cops always had it in for Paulie, anyway. The drugs in his pocket belonged to that tramp girlfriend. Paulie was just holding them so she wouldn't get high. He was doing her a favor. He was a good boy, really he was.

When she took a breath, I asked, "How's Big Paul dealing with it?" I liked her husband, a friendly, funny guy who always manned the grill at the parties they threw in their backyard.

"Who cares?" she said with venom. I tried to remember if she and Big Paul had gotten divorced, if I had somehow missed that part of their lives. "Who cares how that fucking degenerate gambler feels about anything?" She rattled on for another ten minutes, but I didn't hear another word after *degenerate gambler.*

Why was she so forgiving of Paulie and so harsh toward his father? I wanted to tell her that I had recently read where a UCLA psychiatrist claimed that gambling is a brain disease, in the same way as other addictions. Is it because there's no bottle or needle, no visible crutch? Did she think Big Paulie was weak because he was a gambler, and could control it if only he had backbone?

◆ ◆ ◆

A few weeks later I drove down to an affluent suburb just north of Manhattan. I arrived early, and sat in my car in a church parking lot, wondering how many people might show up. It was raining and cold and it would have been the perfect night to blow off a meeting like this. I was already thinking I shouldn't have come. It had been a long time since I had played poker online, but I was curious to see what had changed in those years. Online gambling was in the news almost every day.

At ten to seven, cars started pulling into the lot, and by seven you couldn't get a spot. People were driving around the neighborhood, parking on the street.

I waited until everyone was already inside, and then I slipped in and tried to plaster myself against the back wall. I was the only one standing. There were about sixty people in the room, a third of them women. Everyone was nicely dressed. I looked around, and locked eyes with a boy who could not have been more than fifteen. His face was marked with acne. He smiled, but I didn't return it. He motioned to the empty chair next to him. I hesitated, and then shook my head, no. He looked away quickly.

The man who led the meeting read a short story, and then said that it was a big night because there were two anniversaries. A woman came to the podium. She was five feet tall and probably weighed three hundred pounds. "My name is Ella, and I'm a compulsive gambler." Everyone said hello back to her.

Ella told us how for the past ten or twelve years she was too embarrassed to go out of the house, because of her weight. But she loved gambling, so she would schlep down to Atlantic City every month or so, the one place where nobody cared how heavy she was. "And then one day I was on the Internet and saw that I could play blackjack online." Ella didn't leave her house for two years. She lost tens of thousands of dollars, but at least people weren't staring. "And then my daughter went into labor with my first grandchild. We had planned that I would meet her and her husband at the hospital, but I didn't go to see my Cody being born because I was having a good day and I thought I could win back all that money."

Of course she lost even more, and her daughter decided she wouldn't let Ella see the new baby until she got some help. "It took me another year," Ella confessed, "but finally I came here. It's been six months, and day by day I feel stronger. Thank you." Ella was given some kind of coin, and slowly made it back to her chair.

Then the young kid stood up and walked to the podium. I was shocked—I'd assumed he was there with a family member, supporting *their* addiction. "I'm Zach," he said shyly, "and I'm a compulsive gambler." Zach learned to play poker from his grandmother. "I used to play with my cousins, and then I started playing with the guys in school." They taught him Texas hold'em, and he was good. Very good. One of the kids showed him how you could play online.

"I stole my grandma's credit card and started playing every night," he said. "I thought about how I was going to buy her a new car, 'cause she drives this crappy Honda. I was going to surprise her and make her so happy." Instead, he kept losing and losing. He didn't know what to do. He charged thousands of dollars on her card, and then he would rush home from school and take the bill out of her mailbox. He would steal money from his grandmother's wallet and from his parents' drawers, stuff the cash in an envelope and send it to the credit card company.

This went on for close to a year, until his grandmother caught him at the mailbox. "She told me how disappointed she was," Zach said, looking like the small boy he really is. "And that was the worst part. She paid off her credit card, and I started coming to these meetings. I want to have a better life. My family loves me so much, and I let them all down. It's been a year today since I gambled. Thank you."

People started clapping, and Zach tucked his head into his shoulder, like a turtle into its shell.

As he walked back to his seat, he caught my eye again. This time I smiled. I went and sat next to him, and put my arm around his shoulder.

I stayed around after the meeting and talked to Zach for a while, and then to some of the adults.

A car pulled up and Zach jumped into the front seat. He leaned over and kissed the driver on the cheek. I saw in the way she touched his face that she was his mother. She turned and gave us a little wave, and we all waved back. I thought about the tsunami of gamblers who were going to wash up in these meetings in the next few years, and about how many of them were going to look like Zach. And like Ella. So many kids, and so many women, drawn in precisely because it's something they can do in front of their computer screens, in private, with no one watching.

Then the outside lights of the church were shut off, and everyone started saying good night.

"Good luck," Ella said as she shook my hand. For the first time, those two words didn't make me feel confused.

"Good luck to you, too," I told her sincerely.

◆ ◆ ◆

Sometimes I am approached by people in my town, asking me if I'll teach their teenagers to play poker. They've heard I'm good, and know about the fun I used to have with the poker kids. I don't tell them how much I fret about those boys, and how sometimes I wish I had never invited them over for those pizza dinners and poker lessons, despite the laughter and fun we had. What if one of them already had the "addiction gene" and that lethal combination of fun, food, and gambling that I grew up around rears its head and strikes in a way I can't even imagine, taking them down a path that looks like the road to paradise, but instead leads them straight to hell? I always decline.

But I have never stopped playing poker in my Wednesday-night game. Even during the worst of Paradise, and the best of being away from it, I was thrilled to be with my buddies each week. A few new guys started playing with us, and the game has become more entertaining. We're boisterous and convivial, rarely arguing.

I know that Tommy, the man from my first Gamblers Anonymous meeting, would tell me I was going down a slippery slope, that gambling is gambling. But I don't see it that way. On Wednesday night I don't care if I win or lose, although my buddies would point out that's because I win most weeks. But this game is social and relaxing, not compulsive and fearful. It reminds me of the fun that I had when I first started playing, and how much I love poker. And it shows me that I'm no longer out of control, fighting a dragon I could never slay.

♦ ♦ ♦

I am such a coward. So many times over the years I had a chance to tell Steve, my family, and my friends what had happened, how my life had been hijacked to Paradise. I never did.

Instead I sent them this manuscript. I did it incrementally. First to Michael. Would he ever play poker with me again? Would he want to turn away? "You poor baby," he said the next morning. "It must have been hell."

That gave me the courage to give it to Keith and Barbie. I expected them to be angry with me, disappointed. Instead, Keith called and said, "Why didn't you ever tell me? You must have been so afraid."

I sent it to Helene and Harvey with a note. *I'm so sorry,*

it read. They called the next afternoon. "Mommy would be so proud of you," they both said. I wept. "Thank god," my sister added, "that Mommy died before she found out she could play slots online."

Next to some of my friends—Valerie Fanarjian, Rya Kihlstedt, and Gil Bellows, people who had known me during my foray into Paradise, who had asked over and over if I was okay. People I had lied to and told that they didn't know what they were talking about. Every one of them called me back to say that they wished I had told them, that they wished they could have helped.

All of them asked when I was going to show it to Steve.

I truly thought I would die before that happened. I couldn't imagine how it would play out. Finally I had no choice.

The note to Steve said, *This is the hardest thing I have ever had to do.*

Steve read it at his shop. I went home and cried myself sick.

I waited for him to come home and was sure that he would tell me that he was leaving me, that he hated me, that he couldn't look at me anymore.

And he was infuriated. That's putting it mildly. But after ranting and yelling, breaking my favorite bowl, and asking me a thousand times to tell him exactly how much money I had lost, he put his arms around me and asked if

I was okay. That was the beginning of real forgiveness for myself.

◆ ◆ ◆

Years after I stopped playing poker online, I went to the post office and was handed a large, heavy package. It looked like it had been thrown from a moving car—all the padding was falling out and the return label was torn off. My postmaster laughed when she gave it to me. "It pays to live in a small town," she said, pointing to the illegible address. Only my last name was clear. I tore it open, and found four clear plastic cases, full of gorgeous, heavyweight clay poker chips. Each chip had the Paradise Poker logo— the white sand, the blue, blue sea, that lone palm tree. There was a note, but it was ripped and ringed with stains.

I could imagine what it said, though: *Come back to Paradise.* Maybe they missed me. Maybe they noticed that I hadn't anted up. Of course, that was it. For the briefest of seconds I thought, *Maybe, maybe, maybe.* And just as quickly, I shook it off. Because now I know that paradise is sitting under a palm tree on a gorgeous, secluded beach, watching the waves tickle the sand.

This time, *I* laugh out loud.

♦ ACKNOWLEDGMENTS ♦

It was Academy Awards night, the year I turned ten. I was lying on my parents' king-size bed in my baby-doll pajamas with my sister, Helene, my Aunt Tillie, and my mother. We were eating mini grilled cheese sandwiches, with the crusts cut off. "Just the way they make them in Los Angeles," Aunt Tillie assured us. Right after Elizabeth Taylor won her Best Actress award for *Butterfield 8*, I fluffed my hair and turned to my adoring audience. "I just want to tell you," I said, using my father's shoehorn as a microphone, "I did this all by myself. I have no one to thank." As I took my bow, my sister and Aunt Tillie clapped like mad, but I saw a quick twitch of annoyance cross my mother's face.

As usual my mother was right. I'll be hoarse before I thank everyone who helped me get this mammoth project to fruition.

♦ ♦ ♦

My thanks to:

Steve Heller, for loving me and forgiving me when I couldn't love or forgive myself. For being one of those few great men who make a woman's life better—supportive, loving, and willing to rearrange the furniture every few months. For his innate creativity and hidden smarts. And above all for his wacky sense of humor.

My fabulous agent, Lynn Johnston, who met me for the first time in the noisiest restaurant in Manhattan, and within twenty minutes convinced me *Hats & Eyeglasses* was the book I should write. And then she went and sold it.

My editor, Sara Carder, who was so insightful and respectful, and who forgave me for my idiotic big mouth.

My sister, Helene Rodgville, who shows me every day what I could be—*if* I was a genuinely selfless, caring human being like her. And for telling me over and over how proud my mother would be of me.

My brother-in-law, Harvey Rodgville, who never judged me and gave me so much encouragement, as well as telling me that my disorganization and sloppy nature are to be counted among my assets. I just love this man.

My niece, Mara Jones-Shiflet, and her fantastic husband, Doug Shiflet, who, in their time of crisis, laughed out loud while reading this manuscript.

Alex Jones, who made my mother happy every single day and taught her so much about the world.

Neil and Barbara, who are family in the truest sense. Hope I did you proud.

Valerie Fanarjian, the greatest sidekick, rooting section, and friend anyone could ever hope for.

Gil Bellows, for not letting me take the easy path.

Rya Kihlstedt, Ava Bellows, and Giovanni Bellows, who nurture my spirit in so many many ways.

Randy Finch, for bringing me to poker when I could have just gone with my stupendous career. What a bore that would have been.

Brendan Edwards, for helping me deforest the planet. And doing it with such good humor.

Rosie Flanders, for making me dig deeper. And deeper still.

The late, great Chris Flanders, who could fill any room with his wonderful, infectious laugh. And for teaching me the real Pythagorean theorem. I was so honored to be one of his "gals."

Margie and Jeff Bauml, whose generosity has always

amazed me, and who let me be godmother to their kids, a job I took more seriously than Michael Corleone.

Carl Bauml, have I ever told you about the day you were born? I've adored you since then. Oh, maybe you should skip Chapter 2, kiddo.

Molly Bauml, my favorite New York to L.A. companion since she was eight, for her keen eye and for being so entertaining. And for never telling a soul about that dented red Mustang.

All my friends who kept me fed and laughing during this arduous process—Chrissy and Charlie DeBellis, Ben and Kari Mack, January DeBellis, Janina DeBellis, Nick Formont, and Bruce Taylor. Those two princelets, Noah Leader and Elias Formont, for letting me hang with you. And Sharon Burns-Leader, for teaching me about Swanee River.

Tory Ettlinger, gracious under fire, generous, and truly encouraging, even in her own hard times.

Fred Goldfrank, who was never afraid of taking the hard way. Our own rocket scientist. Missed every day.

Author Lynn Biederman, who fell into my life just when I was unraveling. NBFF, eagle-eyed reader, and finder of all things inconsistent. You are my serendipity.

Ellen Chenoweth, who is going to make me read this whole book out loud to her. Which I will do with good humor, I swear.

Jamie Midgley, for being such a supportive Brit.

Susan Brown and Linda Atkins, who believed in me so firmly.

Dan Leader and everyone at Bread Alone; Rosie Burgher and those great women at the Olive Free Library; and the rest of my wonderful little town, who have been asking me for the last decade or so when the hell I was finally going to finish this book.

Mike Karpf, for always keeping Steve focused.

Andrea Hameed, for her early reading, one gambler's daughter to another.

I always wanted to be part of a team, and while I dreamt it would be the Yankees, I have found a real home with the Tarcher team—Shanta Small, Jen Levy, and Kat Obertance, who answered my endless questions with unfailing good humor. And the amazing Amanda Dewey for the wonderful design, and Ben Gibson for the dreamy cover.

Esther Ratner, the most amazing researcher—if you told me I was a tall redhead from the South, I'd believe y'all.

The New York Foundation for the Arts, for the gift of money.

The MacDowell Colony, for all that delicious solitude, and for giving me the luxury of time.

SUNY Ulster's artist-in-residence program, for making

this college dropout feel so clever and smart. Larry Berk, you are so missed.

All the people I've played poker with over the years— Joe, Linda, Herbie, Barry, Jay, Bruce, Bob, Robert, and Lenny.

The poker kids—Nick Goldfrank, Nels Leader, Jack Wasylyk, and David Zeines, now such fine men. I learned way more from you than you from me. I still have that paper plate with "the list" on it.

Doug "Foodini" Grunther, Larry "Slide" Silver, James "Jimbo" Robinson, and Randy "I Raise" Burgess, for making me laugh till seltzer shoots out of my nose, and for letting me so happily be your Eva Braun and Frau Blücher.

And especially Michael Miller, who seduced me into falling in love with poker in the first place. Not to mention buying me my lucky tiara.

I owe everything to the spectacular Annie Flanders— friend, mentor, editor. Every word of this book is better because of her. As is every day of my life. If you're ever floundering and don't know what direction your life should take, Annie is your go-to girl.

For the past twenty years, Martha Frankel has been traveling around the world, interviewing actors, writers, and musicians, including J. J. Abrams, Ray Carver, Robert De Niro, Leonardo DiCaprio, Janet Jackson, Angelina Jolie, Spike Lee, Sean Penn, and Elizabeth Taylor.

Her work has appeared in magazines as diverse as *The New Yorker*, *Movieline's Hollywood Life*, *Cosmopolitan*, Japanese *Vogue*, *Nippon*, and the original *Details*.

Frankel has been an on-air contributor to VH1's "Sexiest Movie Moments," *Entertainment Tonight*, and *Inside Edition*.

She is the co-host of Doug Grunther's *The Woodstock Roundtable*, a Sunday-morning radio talk show, broadcast

on WDST in Woodstock, New York, and on demand at
www.wdst.com.

Since the inception of the Woodstock Film Festival
in 2000, Frankel has been the moderator of the Actors
Dialogue. Among the actors who have participated in
these panels are Steve Buscemi, Olympia Dukakis, Stanley
Tucci, Marcia Gay Harden, and Aidan Quinn.

She is a winner of a NYFA award in creative nonfiction,
was the 1997 Philip Morris Fellow at The MacDowell Colony, and the 2003 Artist-in-Residence at SUNY Ulster.

Frankel is hard at work on her first novel.

Visit her website at: www.marthafrankel.com.